RESTO-MOD
MUSCLE CARS

Bill Holder and

D1294270

©2008 Bill Holder and Phil Kunz

Published by

krause publications

An Imprint of F+W Publications

**700 East State Street • Iola, WI 54990-0001
715-445-2214 • 888-457-2873
www.krausebooks.com**

Our toll-free number to place an order or obtain
a free catalog is (800) 258-0929.

Library of Congress Control Number: 2007940898

ISBN-13: 978-0-89689-616-1
ISBN-10: 0-89689-616-1

Designed by Paul Birling
Edited by Tom Collins

Printed in China

ACKNOWLEDGMENTS

COMPANIES

AutoKraft Race Cars and Restoration .... Kurt Anderson
Baker's Vintage Automotive .... Brian Baker
Blue Moon Motorsports .... Al Kamhi
Dynamic Motorsports Superformance .... Jim Gander
Engine Factory, Inc. .... Christian Nelson
Fesler Productions .... Chris Fesler
G-Force Design Concepts, LLC .... John Brooks
Galpin Auto Sports .... Steve Carpenter
Grant Products .... Tom Terr
Hasty's Car Country .... James Hasty
Hills Classic Cars .... Melody McKay
Hot Rod Construction .... Dan Wickett
Just Dream'n .... Russ Tilks
K.A.R. Auto Group .... George Waydo
Kruse International .... Sarah Daily
Lattoff Chevrolet .... Mike Morgan
Modern Muscle .... Dave Weber
n2a Motors .... Gene Langmesser
Performance West
Redline Autosport .... Jefferson Bryant
Reenmachine .... Pete Waydo
Saleen .... Mike Haas
Schwartz Extreme Performance .... Jeff Schwartz
Turn Key Auto Supply
Ultimate Customs
Unique Performance .... Kristen Boozer
YearOne .... Brad Ocock and Pat Staton
Yenko-Wildfire .... Bill Rea

INDIVIDUALS

Justin Baker, Al Baury, Chuck Butts, Wayne Carrier, Scott Dallis, Gene Flaugher,
Calvin Fleek, Jimm Haessly, Chuck Hamly, Pat and Tom Harber, Dave Harper,
Jim Hostottle, Barry Kaminski, Jeff Kuhn, Randy Mack, Raymond May, Tom Merkt
Todd Miller, Robert Motz, Willy Murray, Alan Nichols, Rick Parsons,
Rod Prather/Jeannine Roll, Matt Ray, Dave Rudy, John Scherer, Ken Sarbu, Okey Smith,
Dennis Vanderhoff, Woward West, John Whip and Jason Wyrick.

RESTO-MOD
MUSCLE CARS

FOREWORD

Don't look now, but the recycled muscle-car movement has just shifted from third to fourth gear. Granted, every time any of us restores a muscle car we're recycling it, in the sense that something formerly used up gets a new life.

In the past few years, a number of manufacturers have started producing their own versions of the supercars that once rolled forth from performance-minded dealers like Yenko Chevrolet and Royal Pontiac. But these new-generation supercars are amped-up beyond what even Yenko or Royal ever contemplated back when they were super-tuning Detroit muscle back in the 1960s.

But these new recyclables are not clones, exactly. Most started life as base-model Camaros, Mustangs, Chevelles, etc., but were made into something that's part traditional muscle car and part custom street machine. They were stripped down to the last nut and bolt and rebuilt with the latest suspension pieces, modern interiors and honkin' V-8s.

There were a number of names for these unique machines, but today they can best be described using the "Resto-Mod" nomenclature.

Many of these resto machines are one-offs and produced either in the owner's garage or by one of a number of rod shops across the nation.

That's one aspect of the hobby, but there is also a low-level series production aspect to consider. Unique Performance, for example, manufactures continuation models for both Shelby and Foose, with various resto models of 1960s Shelby Mustangs and Foose Camaros. In addition, Baldwin-Motion is recreating its late-series Camaros. Also, Mr. Norm is involved in the Resto-Mod process with his 1968 Hemi GSS Darts.

As much of the hobby uses vintage donor cars, the demand for this sheet metal continues to grow along with the prices they are commanding. Many of the donor bodies are in poor condition. Guess it's not surprising that there are several companies that are fabricating repo bodies with excellent accuracy.

Recycling muscle in this fashion really represents a new direction, and shows that even this hobby, mature as it is, still spins off fresh trends and products.

It all makes us wonder what's next!

STEVE STATHAM
Editor, *Musclecar Enthusiast Magazine*
musclecarenthusiast.com

CHAPTER 1

DEFINING THE RESTO-MOD

This 1957 Chevrolet Bel Air two-door hardtop in Resto-Mod guise shows the talented enthusiast can bring a new style out of a timeless look. Wheels, paint, interior and more are all new features. John Gunnell

The name game with this class of modified cars is confusing to say the least. There are a multitude of nicknames that describe, or closely describe, the manner of the modification.

The names vary from Pro-Touring, Retro-Mod, Resto-Rod, Retro-Rod, Continuation, Replica Cars, Replicas, Recreations, Hybrids, and on and on.

But for the purposes of this book, we'll use what seems to be the most popular overall nomenclature. The term is **Resto-Mod,** and it best describes the work that is accomplished on these cars.

First, the "Resto" term refers to the vintage look of these cars. The popularity of the body designs of the performance cars of the 1950s, 1960s and 1970s is the external look that many of these cars demonstrate. And 99 percent of the time, the sheet metal remains unaltered except for some smoothing and removal of some or all of the chrome.

The "Mod" portion of the name could understandably have two meanings, but the most meaningful use of the word identifies the modern aspect of the Resto-Mod machines.

A familiar resto logo, the pesky Super Bee of the 1960s, has returned to modern Dodge performance machines.

Modern in this application points to the modernization of the power train, suspension, interior, wheels and tires, and usually in the paint scheme. But you could also use the "Modified" interpretation because there certainly is a lot of modification here.

The Shelby cars of the 1960s have been recreated by Carroll Shelby in the 2000s. Here are two of the modern GT-500E Resto-Mods. *Ford Motor Co.*

A huge resto fan, Jay Leno beams when he views the resto 2009 Camaro. *GM*

Of course, the level of modification in Resto-Mods varies with each example. Some Resto-Mods reach the level of outlandish and some are done very minimally. It's very difficult to discern the level of modification viewing them from the exterior.

But before going further, it would be appropriate to actually give the general ground rules that define a Resto-Mod. Now remember, there is nothing rock-solid in this hobby, but here is our best attempt to lay out the rules that generally apply to these machines.

1. The older body used should be the original or consist of an assembly of parts that provides a close-to-stock look. Many Resto-Mods have had their bodies smoothed out with slight changes to the factory curves, along with having door handles, trim and emblems removed.

2. It goes without saying that no body chopping, channeling, or tubbing of the rear end is in the spirit of the Resto-Mod concept. Also, the cutting of a hole in the hood to fit a protruding tunnel ram or supercharger set-up doesn't work either.

3. The power train for many of the 1960s and '70s Resto-Mods is a totally modern arrangement. In some cases, the power plant is a built-up-style engine. It should be noted with Resto build-ups of 1930s and 1940s models that many of the engines are not new, but are still much newer than the bodies that are sitting above them. Many times the engines and transmissions are three to four decades newer.

4. In order to continue the modern look, the interiors of most Resto-Mods have been updated with custom

Not only are modern engines used in Resto-Mods, but their appearance sometimes is awe-inspiring. It looks like it could power the Star Ship Enterprise!

seats, door panels, headliners, a new dashboard and instruments, a steering column and wheel, and on and on. Some of the restorations have all those upgrades done, while some Restos might delete one or two of them.

5. Many have larger wheels. A trend that started on street machines has found its way into Resto-Mods. The normal 15- and 16-inch wheels used on most cars are removed on Resto-Mods. Many of them carry wheels with diameters up to 18 inches and, on occasion, as large as 20 inches.

6. Upgraded suspension, brakes, and chassis. In this category, the changes range from complete with custom chassis to just minor changes.

The Resto-Mod concept is manifested in an interesting way with the "restofication" of the new production muscle cars of the early 21st century.

Three prime examples of this phenomenon are the 2007 Shelby GT-500 Mustang, the 2008 Dodge Challenger and the 2009 Chevy Camaro.

All three of these haulers sport bodies that mimic their muscle counterparts of the 1960s.

There is certainly no mistaking that muscle look that remains insanely popular today. And, of course, the remainder of the car is state-of-the-art and beyond. Viewing these production machines for the first time, it would

be hard to imagine that they weren't Resto-Mods built by some sophisticated custom rod shop. With those stock-appearing 1960s-style bodies and all the modern upgrades, they fulfill all the Resto-Mod ground rules!

For many baby boomers, the 1960s and '70s muscle cars were the cars of their dreams, and for most part, the cars were something that they certainly couldn't afford at the time. But today, when those cars are in restored states and are rolled onto the auction block, they are even less affordable now than 40 years earlier.

Certain models are bringing in the high six-figure range, and in a small number of cases, in the millions of dollars at national auctions.

Of course, many of these models are rare and brilliantly restored, which gives them the look of a fine piece of jewelry. Guess it goes without saying that a majority of these machines are rarely driven and many languish in garages, car displays and museums.

But what about the others that enjoy the sport? Those decades-old cars have an appeal to them, but they need to be experienced in a different manner.

The classic bodies and the remaining portions of those cars are 40-or-more years old, and the power trains, suspension and all the other parts and pieces are of that long-ago technology level.

Finding parts for these stock muscle cars continues to be a more difficult procedure as the years go by. And if you do locate that Tri-Power carb set-up that you've just got to have, you are going to pay for it until it hurts.

But how about the Resto-Mod that retains the look of your long-lusted-for model, but with everything modern under the skin? Right off the bat, there's the increased performance, safety, and certainly the greater reliability that is provided.

Besides the startling looks of the Resto-Mod from the outside, the modern performance power trains are compatible with the current unleaded fuels and do not require valve seat hardening and other engine modifications.

There certainly isn't an infinite supply of 1960s/1970s muscle car bodies. There are a number of companies building resto bodies. These are Camaros, many of which will find their way into Resto-Mod creations. *Dynacorn*

Custom Resto-Mods are very much a hand-built operation with each being a one-of-a-kind. Here, a 1950s Chevy receives a modern performance engine.

This professionally built 1965 Mustang demonstrates a popular model for this type of restoration. It includes a modern engine, upgraded interior and suspension, while retaining the original body.

Ohio Resto-Mod retailer Jim Hasty explained that the Resto-Mod is something that can be driven. "If something breaks in the modern engine under the hood, there are parts available for repair. If that were to happen to an original high-dollar muscle car, a replacement part price would be out of sight, if you could find one. And if you did have to put in a non-original part, it would hurt the value of the car.

"Also, most of those vintage big blocks require special high-performance fuel which makes them very expensive and impractical to drive," Hasty explained.

In addition, with the modern suspension, large modern wheels, and larger tires of most Resto-Mods, there is a better ride. And how about having huge four-wheel disc brakes to stop your 3,500-pound hauler instead of what was available back in the 1960s?

The Resto-Mod-type large tires and wheels have been around for some time, and are the only changes that are made to many vintage machines. It does make one wonder whether a particular vehicle seen from a distance is indeed a Resto-Mod.

Certainly a Resto-Rod has a great look and performance to burn from rompin,' stompin,' injected big blocks, many capable of up to 450-to-500 horsepower. But as neat as they look, they usually don't approach the value of a totally restored version of the original model. But it is surprising to learn how much money they sometimes attract. For example, in a recent national auction, a Resto-Mod 1970s Hemi 'Cuda brought home more than $80,000!

A modernization of those major systems, yet retaining the vintage look of the machine, is a trend that has really caught on. It's a technique that was accomplished earlier with 1930s Ford coupes with modern engines being turned into classic hot rods. Later, models would be modernized into street rods and street machines.

But with the 1950s, 1960s and 1970s muscle models, making that kind of conversion gets that Resto-Mod name. Basically, when you think about it, the Resto-Mod could be defined as a hybrid vehicle with its vintage body lines and modern performance technology.

An interesting reminder of the Resto-Mod concept can be seen in the toy stores and model shops. A great majority of the 1950s through 1970s models are sporting a Resto-Mod look with big wheels and tires and modern power plants under the hood.

The beauty of the Resto concept is that any model can be used. It can be a six-cylinder Plain Jane model of the car. It doesn't make any difference what the VIN number or the paperwork might be or whether it's a numbers-matching car. It even renews the junkyard searching to find a classic body hiding at the bottom of a stack of cars.

Guess it's not surprising that you see ads in trade magazines offering "good money" for any-condition 1960s and 1970s Camaros, Chevelles, Mustangs and the like. You can figure out what many of those folks often have planned for them.

In the reverse situation, individuals selling those type of cars sometimes indicate in their advertisements, "Would make a great Resto-Mod!"

But there isn't an infinite supply of those bodies, and sometime in the near future, they will be extremely difficult to locate and expensive to acquire. There is, however, a modern way of getting around that situation.

A number of companies, such as Dynacorn and Goodmark, can provide complete bodies for popular 1960s models such as the Camaro and Mustang in exact factory specs.

One Resto-Mod builder said that he really likes to use those new bodies. "They come in perfect condition with no dents or dings needing to be repaired. But most importantly, there isn't any rust to have to deal with."

Another positive characteristic of this hobby is that there is a substantial interest in Resto-Mods from the younger set. It goes without saying that most of these hobbyists were not born when the first Mustang hit the dealership floors in 1964.

The August 2007 Car Craft *magazine cover indicated how popular the Resto-Mod phenomenon has become.*

And it's those classic 1964 through 1966 'Tangs that have generated a huge interest in that portion of the population. And in the largely unwritten and very change-able rules of Resto-Mod construction, most of those classic bodies are left in the same configuration they had when they left the Ford production lines so long ago.

But the point should be that almost every Resto-Mod, with the exception of the low-number production models, is a one-off vehicle—custom-made by the owner or for

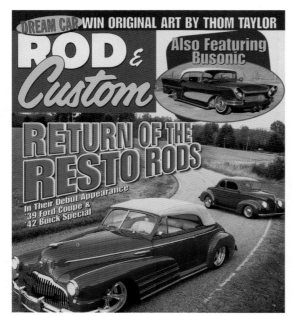

In their May 2005 issue, Rod and Custom *proclaimed the "Return of the Resto Rods" with exciting versions of the 1939 Ford Coupe and a 1942 Buick Special convertible.*

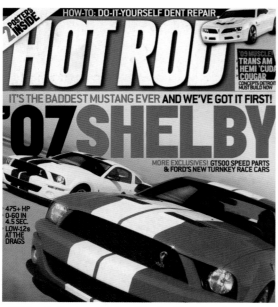

Adding to the popularity of Resto-Mods has been the return of factory-sponsored favorites like this 2007 Shelby Mustang.

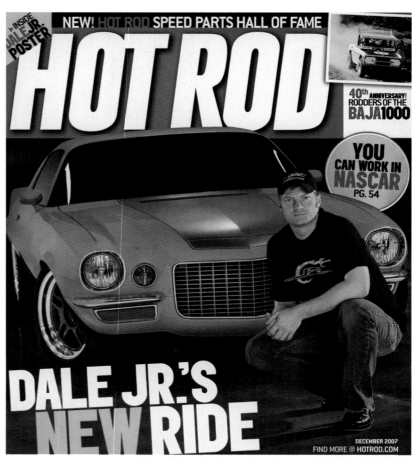

In their December 2007 issue, Hot Rod *showed off the 1972 Rest-Mod Camaro made for NASCAR driver Dale Earnhardt Jr.*

the owner. It's really one step beyond what has been known as street machines for a number of years.

The Resto-Mod concept has been carried forward by a number of aftermarket companies such as Baldwin-Motion, Unique Performance, Foose, Shelby and others who have built small numbers of continuation cars for sale. Most of these companies use original cars as the starting point for their Resto machines.

The Big-Three car builders realize the popularity and excellence of this particular class of

Resto-Mods and some are actually sold in factory dealerships.

There are even Resto-Mod drag cars being constructed by the original builders, such as "Mr. Norm"—Norm Kraus—of Grand Spaulding Dodge in Chicago. He is recreating his famous '68 GSS Hemi Dodge Darts. There are even Resto altered-wheelbase cars being produced.

And, of course, there are many Resto-Mods that are constructed after hours in garages across the nation by muscle car enthusiasts. Many of the models reach a high level of craftsmanship.

It all sounds good, but there are some detractors that completely disagree with the Resto-Mod activity. One muscle car fan indicated that the Resto-Mod folks are destroying every part of the classic cars except the sheet metal and replacing all the rest of the car with modern stuff.

That was one person's thought, but it must be noted that practically none of the true muscle cars are used in these conversions. Only time will tell on how it all plays out, but many feel that there is room for every version of the muscle car hobby.

There were tens of thousands of 1960s and 1970s Barracudas, Novas, and Chevelles produced that weren't Hemi Cudas, SS 396s, or SS 454s. They would have been grabbed up by collectors but were just plain passenger cars. For the most part, the same bodies were used for the six-cylinder versions. That certainly didn't hurt their use in a Resto-Mod build-up.

A measure of the increasing popularity of the Resto-Mod concept certainly was brought to light in August 2007 when two popular national automotive magazines, *Car Craft* and *Muscle Car Enthusiast* had Resto-Mods adorning their covers. *Car Craft's* cover announced, "Resto-Mods You Can Do," while *Muscle Car Enthusiast* projected, "Resto-Mods: Plan It, Build It, Drive It."

There's Mr. October himself, Reggie Jackson, leaning on his pride-and-joy '69 Resto-Mod Camaro. *GM*

T he attraction of the Resto-Mod has found its way into the celebrity ranks with Reggie Jackson, Jay Leno, Dale Earnhardt Jr. and Burt Reynolds all being involved with them.

Reggie Jackson's 1969 Camaro Resto-Mod

The retired New York Yankee superstar, known as "Mr. October" for his hitting prowess in many World Series games for the Yankees as well as the Oakland A's, has had a magnificent collection of muscle cars for a number of years. With the '69 Camaro being one of his all-time favorites, he wanted to build a Resto-Mod version of the car that closely retained the external look of the classic Bowtie.

It all came together when Reggie and GM Performance Parts hooked up. The project also enabled GM to introduce its new LSX engine in a significant manner. Externally, there was no doubt that Reggie was involved, with a logo bearing his autograph and a baseball player swinging the bat silhouetted over a checkered flag pattern. It is located on both the hood scoop and the rear spoiler. The Resto was painted a new shade called Concept Camaro Red.

The LSX logo was also all over the car. And well it should have been since the monster big block pounds down 641 horsepower on the dyno. It's hooked to a six-speed Tremec-built tranny with a Moser-built GM rear end.

This beautiful big-block LSX Chevy is the power for the Jackson Camaro, providing well into the 600-horse range. *GM*

Detroit Speed & Engineering provided the suspension system that featured coil-overs on the front. The rear leaf springs were moved inward to accommodate the larger tires.

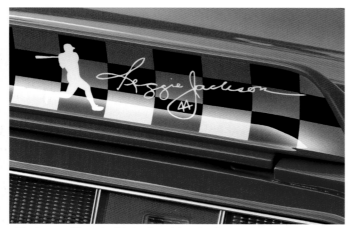

That same "Reggie-Racing" emblem is also on the rear of the rear deck spoiler. *GM*

That's the new engine for the Toronado, which is a super upgrade to a Cadillac CTS power plant that is pounding down over 1,000 ponies. *GM*

The interior has somewhat of a factory look, but it's obvious that there are considerable custom parts and pieces. In addition, it sports custom black-spoke wheels.

It's really something to behold!

JAY LENO'S 1966 OLDSMOBILE TORONADO RESTO-MOD.

Another famous collector of exotic automobiles, comedian Jay Leno, has a Resto-Mod of amazing proportions. This creation was derived from an unlikely front-wheel-drive machine, the 1966 Oldsmobile Toronado.

But in its Resto-Mod configuration, the vehicle was converted to rear-wheel-drive. And like the Jackson Camaro, it retains much of its original external looks. That's where the similarity ends.

Under that large hood rests 1,070 horsepower coming from a modified Cadillac CTS-V racing engine. The engine can get up to 7,000 rpm at a compression ratio of 8.3-1 and drives 17-inch tires.

Interior-wise, it's pretty stock. But there are some changes on the dashboard. Also, other aspects of the vehicle have been upgraded.

Leno shows some interested onlookers the hows and whys of his Toronado's power plant. *GM*

The 1966 Toronado of Jay Leno might look pretty stock, but that certainly isn't the case. The Resto-Mod had to be converted from front-to-rear wheel drive. *GM*

That's the new Resto-Mod version of the new YearOne "Smokey and the Bandit" Trans Am. This posed photo shows a lawman in close pursuit, a position that Burt Reynolds often found himself in during those popular movies. YearOne

That's the Bandit's logo which rests on the dash of the "Smokey and the Bandit" Trans Am. YearOne

BURT REYNOLDS AND THE 1977-'79 "BANDIT" TRANS AM RESTO-MODS

Unlike the Jackson and Leno Resto-Mods, which were both one-of-a-kind, this model will be produced by YearOne in several versions. These Resto-Mods are addressed in Chapter 3.

But be assured, this is the Resto-Mod version of the Trans Am that Reynolds made famous in the classic "Smokey and the Bandit" movies of the 1970s and 1980s.

THE DALE EARNHARDT JR. CAMARO RESTO-MOD

NASCAR driver Dale Earnhardt Jr. chose a 1972 Camaro set up like a period Trans Am racer for his Resto-Mod ride. Detroit Speed and Engineering (DSE) of Monroeville, N.C., got the job. Included in the package was a DES sub frame kit and rear suspension system with a GM LS2 crate engine putting out 440 hp and coupled to a T56 six-speed automatic. Painted Sherwin Williams Planet Orange, Earnhardt's Camaro has brake cooling ducts where turn signals once functioned. Inside is an I-Pod-ready stereo, a roll bar and a rear seat shelf for his dog set over a subwoofer and 6 x 9-inch speakers. Hope Rover likes music! *(See photo on page 12)*

CHAPTER 2

MODERN RESTO INFLUENCE

The new Mustangs use the identical design that appeared on the original Mustangs.

The influence of the muscle-car era of the 1960s and 1970s is hard to kick. In fact, in the 21st century it seems that it's stronger than ever.

It was an era when body styling with vertical front ends was far more important than the design that would decrease aerodynamic drag and increase fuel economy. Of course, there were those 400-plus-cubic-inch, big-block V-8 engines that were pounding down unbelievable horsepower and torque. Heck, gas prices were only about 30 cents a gallon, so who cared?

Starting in the 1970s, with the gas crunch and the increased insurance costs for high performance models, all the cars started to look the same. Starting near the end of last century there were some clues that the Big-Three

The "GT" Ford nickname from the 1960s has come back on modern Mustangs.

The Mach 1 Mustang of the 1960s was a top pony-car performer. It's not surprising that the name has reappeared in modern times.

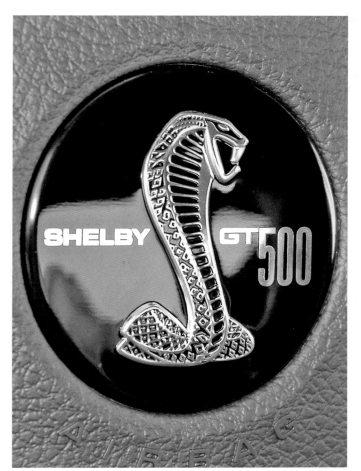

The center cap of the steering wheel of the '07 GT-500 Shelby shows the resto Cobra snake.

The famous "427" number, designating engine displacement, has reappeared in Roush aftermarket Mustangs.

The 2007 GT500 Shelby brought that famous designation of Carroll Shelby cars of the 1960s.

company designers were starting to feel that nostalgic pull from both the youth and baby boomer markets.

Really, though, there was one model of the 1960s that had continued to be available through the years in the form of the powerful Ford Shelby Cobra sports car. Few numbers of the machine that brought Ford back to the top of international road racing were produced.

Guess you could really call it the first Resto-Mod as a number of aftermarket builders recreated the car in amazing resemblance to the real thing. These reproduction vehicles have continued to evolve, adding modern technology in suspension systems, engines and other areas.

More recently, there have been hints of the past in modern models. For example, the early-2000s Chevy SSR

The longstanding Chevrolet Super Sport (SS) emblem of the 1960s has made it back to 2000s model.

The front end of the 2000s Chevy SSR custom truck featured a resto-style grille reminiscent of 1950s-vintage pick-up trucks.

The old "Super Bee" name has been updated for modern Dodge trucks with this "Rumble Bee" emblem.

sport pickup truck carries a grille design that looks very much like the grille of early-1950s Chevy pick-ups.

Also, the current Chevy Impala carries large round taillights that are almost identical to those of the Chevelle of the early 1970s.

The famous model names and abbreviations are starting to appear again on new models. Many of them are appearing in the same lettering styles and sizes. The following are some of that oh-so-familiar nostalgic muscle-car nomenclature:

For Mopar: Charger, Chrysler 300, Daytona, Demon, Hemi and R/T.

For Ford: Boss, Cobra, Cobra Jet and Mach 1.

For Chevy: Super Sport

Although not a pure-production model, a collaboration between Saleen and the legendary Parnelli Jones produced a recreation of the famous number 15 Trans Am Mustang that won the series championship. The recreation used a 2007 Mustang adorned in the correct bright orange color and the characteristic Boss 302 stripes on the sides and body center.

That modern Resto racing machine goes much further than just the appearance package since the pair were actually owner and driver of the actual Trans Am machine. That relationship is carried through to this model as every buyer of the 500 produced will have the dash autographed by both men.

To a lesser degree, another aftermarket modification of the modern Mustang was accomplished by the Unique

A number of earlier remembrances are visible on the rear of this 2007 Monte Carlo. In addition to the SS emblem are the Super Stock-style stripes and the large, round taillights from 1970s-era Malibus.

Performance/Chip Foose organization with its Stallion model. Although the detailing is not totally authentic when compared with early muscle Mustangs, the flashy model sports 1960s accents with modified Boss-style side stripes and a characteristic twin-stripe arrangement on the hood.

The 2003 Mercury Marauder brought back a famous racing name of the early 1960s when the model was a dominant runner in NASCAR.

2003 MERCURY MARAUDER

In 2003, Mercury brought back a famous 1960s name with its Marauder model. That brand name epitomized both NASCAR racing and performance V-8s for Mercury customers during the 1960s. Reportedly, the Marauder was supposed to be a Ford model but was switched over to the Mercury brand late in the design phase.

A little-known fact was that the original Marauder could be bought off the showroom floor with a monster 427 big block along with the Interceptor 390, as well as the Super 390 V-8s.

Again, it was Parnelli Jones whose name was attached to the model because of his excellent driving successes in those fastback Marauder racing machines.

The modern Marauder was an entirely different beast. It was the performance version of the Mercury Grand Marquis. And even though it didn't have the general appearance (heck, it was a four-door) or the muscular performance aspects of the original, it certainly brought back memories of that former NASCAR hauler blazing down the straightaways of Daytona and Talladega.

There was certainly no mistaking that super-sharp modern Mercury Marauder with that famous name carved into the rear bumper. Unfortunately, it just lasted that single model year.

Although not an exact replica of the earlier T-bird, there were a lot of hints of the model in the 2003 resto-appearing Thunderbird. The same grille design is carried through in the new model. Ford Motor Co.

The power from the supercharged 3.9-liter engine was 280 horses. Ford Motor Co.

2003 FORD (RESTO) THUNDERBIRD

When the 2003 Resto-appearing Thunderbird first debuted, there was great excitement. After all, it was probably the first attempt by the auto industry to produce an authentic Resto-looking production vehicle.

Certainly, there were similarities with that vehicle and the original 1955 through 1957 classic T-Bird two-seaters. But it wasn't nearly as close as the Resto-influenced models that would follow.

There were design cues on the grille, side sheet-metal styling and the rear end. And with the hardtop, those classic well-remembered portholes were in place and increased

The 1957 Thunderbird was the third and final of the two-seat versions and served as the model for the 2003 resto version.

the nostalgic aura of the model. One of the biggest differences with the new model was more of a smoother body design with the headlights and taillight areas being curved downward where the original car had them both vertical. That really made a big change away from the original look and caused some to feel that it looked more like an early 'Vette than a Thunderbird.

The power came from a 3.9 liter V-8 that pumped out 280-horsepower, which was just 20 horses less than the top 300-horsepower supercharged 312 T-Bird engine in the 1957 model.

The Ford GT-40 was a part of the American revolution in world road racing in the 1960s.

2005 - 2007 Ford (Resto) GT

Guess you would have to include the dramatic Ford GT as an ultimate Resto-Mod. Only in this case, it was actually a production vehicle with 4,038 built over three model years.

For anyone with any knowledge of international road racing in the 1960s, there was no doubt that this was indeed a recreation of the GT-40 machine that helped the reputation of American racing.

It certainly wasn't cheap, reaching well into the six-figure category. From a distance, you would swear it's the real thing, but it must be admitted that it is a bit larger than the real McCoy. With this magnificent creation, who's telling?

The resto version of the 1960s Ford GT-40 evolved in the 2000s as the Ford GT. A limited-production vehicle, only 4,038 were built from 2005 through 2007. It would have to be considered the ultimate Resto-Mod!   *Ford Motor Co.*

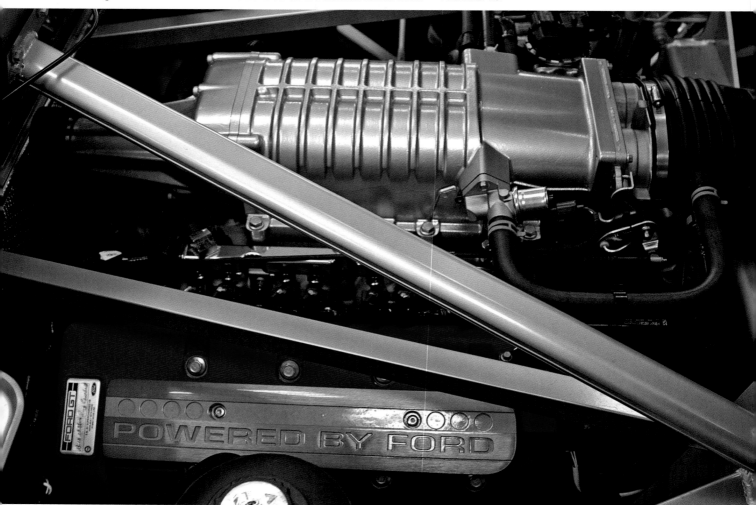

A view of the rear-mounted 5.4-liter, 550 hp engine that drives the Ford GT resto machine.

It should be noted that the GT was actually an aftermarket creation, being completely assembled by Saleen in Troy, MI.

Modern technology abounded in the creation with super-plastic-formed aluminum body panels, bonded floor panels, one-piece door panels and four-piston disc brakes.

The power train was modern in every sense with a supercharged 5.4 liter DOHC 550-horsepower engine. The rotation was handled with a six-speed manual tranny.

In the 1960s, Hertz rented special GT-500Hs from their dealerships. Many of those street rockets were taken to the drag strips. In 2006, a modern resto version of those cars was released carrying the same gold-and-black paint scheme. The models were rented by Hertz and could also be purchased at Ford Dealers. Ford Motor Co.

Probably the most popular Shelby Mustang was the 1967 GT-500.

2007 FORD
(RESTO) SHELBY COBRA GT-500

In most examples, there were hints of the vintage vehicles they remind us of, but with the 2007 Ford Shelby GT-500, there is no doubt what served as the template for the car. Yep, it's the 1967 GT-500.

A bit of history about the 1967 version is the interesting production technique that was carried out. As any Shelby fan will quickly tell you, the earlier GT-500s were completed at a former Shelby production facility in California. Not the case with the 2007, though, as the car is being produced completely by Ford with Carroll Shelby serving in a consulting capacity.

The engines of these same-named haulers were top

gun in each application. For the early version, the power plant of choice was the twin-carbed 428 Super Cobra Jet capable of a factory-announced 335 horsepower. Many will tell you, though, that figure was probably understated.

That was big-time then and this is big-time now. Would you believe 500 horsepower from only 5.4 liters of displacement—only about 330 cubic inches? Are you kidding?

Somebody must have stuck in a purebred racing engine under that stylish hood. It carries the Triton V-8 nametag and has its roots with the GT Supercar engine. Carburetion then, supercharging today — it makes a big difference! Early Ford literature had the horsepower of this screamer at greater than 450, but the figure just kept moving up.

Here's the engine that propelled the Shelby GT-500 into muscle-car history.

The old master himself, Carroll Shelby, stands beside the modern Resto version of his GT-500. *Ford Motor Co.*

Here's a modern resto Mustang in Boss 302 form. Talk about a great Resto-Mod trend!

The 2007 Shelby Cobra GT-500 showed an amazing similarity to the original model.

The body lines are similar, but they appear to be a little pumped up with a more aggressive (maybe even snarling) look and feel about it. Looks like it took the original and fed it steroids!

The wide dual center body stripes scream at you that this is a performance machine. The dominating front-end design features a blackout grille with that ever-present Cobra lurking on the left side. A smaller separate blackout area contains the headlights on either side. Below, the front valance hangs low with a long narrow scoop stretching much of its length. By the way, the "Shelby" name is in place only two times. And the Ford emblem can be found only one time.

A non-protruding pair of scoops are in place in the middle of the hood. In remembrance of that earlier 'Tang, there is that familiar lower body striping with the GT-500 identification contained within, and located on the lower front quarter.

It's definitely got a Resto-Mod look about it with 18-inch tires and classy 10-spoke Ford wheels. There were seven colors offered with the modern GT-500, this example being the popular Torch Red with white racing stripes, but that base color could also have Satin Silver racing stripes. A close-ratio six-speed T-56 Ford tranny accepts the power and sends it down the line to the 3.42-geared rear end.

Although the looks are like the early GT-500, this

The 2007 Shelby Cobra GT-500 brings a great car to a new generation and great memories to those who remember the original.

The supercharged 5.4-liter GT-500 engine is capable of 500 horsepower from only about 330 cubic inches. Totally amazing!

The rear end of the 2007 GT-500 Shelby has a lot of similarities to its original GT-500 counterpart.

machine is certainly a lot weightier than its older brother. Where the 1960s Shelbys weighed in at about 2,600 to 2,700 pounds, this machine is only about 100 pounds short of two tons!

But a test drive of one of the new models quickly shows that those extra ponies under the hood can easily make up for that extra bulk.

The closeness of the ratios of the six-speed are amazing and it seems that there is a smooth acceleration curve while going through the gears. The power from that engine was quite evident, with rubber chirping coming from the first four shifts. The acceleration was unbelievable with each change in gears burying one deeper into the seat. The 2007 Shelby has demonstrated a quarter mile of 13.1 seconds at 119 miles per hour.

The braking is sensational, provided by 14-inch Brembo disc brakes in the front and 11-inchers at the rear.

This 2008 GT-500 re-creates the famous name of the top GT-500 of the day, the GT-500KR—or King of the Road. Ford Motor Co.

The new Challenger was the star of many car shows in 2007. Here, it is displayed on a rotating platform at a show in Dayton, Ohio. A quick look at the body makes one think it is the original sheet metal.

2008 Dodge (Resto) Challenger

Many consider the 2008 Dodge Challenger the best of the factory Resto models. It looks like it just emerged from a custom shop and probably started with a stock 1970 Dodge Challenger body. The initial response from its 2006 exposure to the public verified its amazing external, and internal, appearance.

Granted, there were deviations from the original body style, but the changes that were made were both subtle and pleasing to the eye. It should be remembered that the initial Challenger was built to qualify for the SCCA Trans Am series along with the Plymouth AAR 'Cuda.

The new Challenger certainly fulfills all of its Resto muscle heritage. Under the hood, for example, there's a punchy 6.1-liter Hemi V-8 engine with 425 horsepower at 6,200 rpm. It also has pulling power with 420 lbs.-ft. of torque. It's matched with a six-speed manual tranny.

The engine is a Hemi-powered 6.1-liter V-8 with the famous Hemi name prominently in view. Chrysler

With that potent power train, it's understandable that the acceleration and top-speed capabilities are extremely impressive. For example, try quarter-mile performance in the 13-second-range with just 4.5 seconds to 60 miles per hour and a top speed in the 175 mph range!

With the initial excitement of the Challenger model, one can but wonder if the other super-popular model of the period, the AAR 'Cuda, might receive a similar treatment in the future.

Following the Resto-Mod textbook that Chrysler seemed to use with the Challenger design, the interior was completely modernized with a striking combination of black and grey detailing and aluminum.

As this book was being prepared in the fall of 2007, Chrysler officials announced the first two of the 2008 Dodge Challengers would be auctioned for charity. The Challenger was to make its debut at the Chicago Auto Show in February 2008.

This view of the hood and grille area of the new Challenger has considerable similarities with the real thing. Chrysler

"The Dodge Challenger is an icon," said Mike Accavitti of Dodge marketing. "The revival of this storied nameplate has enthusiasts chomping at the bit to get one."

We couldn't have said it better ourselves. The car of many dreams has returned. Sounds like a match made in Resto-Mod heaven!

The 1969 Camaro SS served as the model for the new resto-style 2009 Camaro. GM

The sweeping lines and rear-quarter simulated vents provide echoes of the earlier Camaro design. GM

2009 CHEVY (RESTO) CAMARO

It was an event that brought great happiness to Bowtie performance fans. After being without the beloved Camaro name since 2002, a concept machine appeared in 2006 during the national auto show season.

It certainly had all the attributes of a Resto-Mod with a body that was close in appearance to the original, and certainly the power train, suspension and interior are all in the modern mode. It was a splashing success and it wasn't surprising that Chevy will also bring forth a convertible model.

No doubt about the body design, which included the classic long-hood/short-rear-deck proportions with the wide rear-tire stance giving the vehicle the look of hugging corners even when sitting still.

Under the long hood is big-time punch with a 400-horsepower, six-liter LS-2 engine, the same one employed in the 'Vette. It's mated to a T56 six-speed manual transmission.

General Motors is betting that this Resto model will grab the attention of the buying public. GM

CHAPTER 3

CONTINUATION AND REPLICAR RESTO-MODS

The Phase III is something else. The standard engine for this speed demon is capable of 600 horsepower and it's possible to acquire up to 1,000 ponies! Paul Zazarine

Where many of the Resto-Mods of today are produced as individual machines by shops or individuals, there is another segment of this Resto movement that looks at the hobby from an entirely different perspective.

It involves the practice of limited-production and identical, or at least very similar, models. Most of these operations use vintage donor bodies as a starting point. Another common denominator is that most have a vintage exterior look and a modernized power train, suspension system and updated interior.

These vehicles go by the names of recreations, continuation cars and other identifications. The companies that produce these unique Resto-Mods are very brand-oriented, with Ford being the dominant brand.

Another interesting characteristic of some of the models is that the builders are actually recreating versions that they built decades earlier. And there are several of these builders that

Here is a period view of the models on the famous Baldwin-Motion showroom floor. These cars served as the basis for the continuation cars that are being built today. Baldwin-Motion

are actually creating Resto-Mod versions of competition vehicles of the 1960s and 1970s.

Here's a look at these interesting operations and their even-more-unique Resto-Mod-style vehicles:

BALDWIN-MOTION CLASSICS

When that famous performance company name comes to mind, it brings back memories of the 1967 through 1974 time period when Joel Rosen fielded his heralded Gen One SS-427 and Phase III Camaros on the nation's drag strips. The Motion-Built big-block Camaros set numerous AHRA and NHRA national records with drivers Rosen, Bill Mitchell and Dennis Ferrara at the wheel.

Well, they are both back in Resto-Mod style, and believe me, they are something else! As Baldwin-Motion describes the new machines: "The SS-427 and Phase III Camaros are contemporary executions of Baldwin-Motion classics, with performance and head-turning power worthy of the iconic brand."

To replicate that great time period, Baldwin-Motion decided in 2006 to recreate a limited number of SS-427 and Phase III versions. The vehicles would be available in Super Sport, Rally Sport and SS/RS trim. They don't come cheap, but if you covet the best, it will cost you $169,000 for the SS-427 and $20,000 more for the Phase III.

Rosen explained that the models are built to customer requirements with an emphasis on quality, fit, finish and of course, performance. Upon completion, each car is performance tested and given a Baldwin-Motion serial number. At press time the plans were to build just a dozen of the cars.

To ensure the identical look of the original cars, the bodies come from donor 1969 Camaro cars. The donors have original 1969 Chevy VIN numbers and can be registered and insured anywhere in the world.

The Super Coupe is powered by an all-aluminum 700-horse Bill Mitchell-built mill. It's 540 cubic inches with 10-1 forged custom pistons, a roller cam and a Kinsler Cross-Ram fuel injection system. The classy big block is capable of 700 horsepower. Paul Zazarine

The Super Coupe is just that—super! The body sports flared fender wells, widened rear fenders, functional brake-cooling scoops, and a functional L-88-style hood. Paul Zazarine

Even though the SuperSpeedster model was built using a 1969 Camaro, there are some deviations from that body. The two tunnels on the rear deck increase in size as they move forward, terminating at the back of the seats. They're encircled with chrome rings. *Paul Zazarine*

The SuperSpeedster engine is a ground-pounding 540-cubic-inch Motion/Merlin mauler that is capable of 700+ horsepower. The all-aluminum engine uses a custom Kinsler Fuel Injection System and a multitude of high-performance upgrades. *Paul Zazarine*

The initial Phase III Camaro is powered by a blueprinted, aluminum-head Kinsler-injected 565-cubic-inch big block and features a five-speed tranny, new Motion IRS rear suspension, eight-piston front and three-piston rear Motion/SSB disc brakes, rack-and-pinion steering, custom red leather interior, an awesome Sony sound system and a host of luxury and performance options.

But there is more! The so-called SuperSpeedster debuted at the 2006 SEMA Show and was one of the stars of the event. It still had the vintage Camaro Resto look, but there were some interesting changes made. Get this: It was a two-seater!

The SuperSpeedster is also based on a '69 Camaro body with power-operated doors along with a fiberglass hood and tonneau cover. Hey, General Motors should have built this car!

The body sits on a tubular-steel chassis with a four-wheel independent suspension system, a Dana 60 limited-slip center section, Penske coil-overs, rack-and-pinion steering and six-piston Baer/Motion disc brakes.

This 2006 artist's conception shows the custom-bodied Super Speedster (yellow car) with the Phase III Camaro in the background. They have been called the ultimate Camaros.
Kris Horton Illustration

The 450-hp SS-427 and 600-hp Phase III are top performers, but there are also both supercharged and twin-turbo big-block mills available that are as large as 720 cubic inches with horsepower values up to an amazing 1,000 ponies!

This Hurst/Grand Spaulding Dodge advertisement displayed an early drawing of how the "Mr. Norm" drag machine would appear.

"MR. NORM'S" 1968 HEMI DART GSS RESTO-MOD

Back in the day (the late 1960s days to be exact) the 1968 Hemi Dart was about the baddest of them all. It was reported that about 80 of the models were sold mostly to drag race teams.

The hauler arrived in primer with the hood and fenders painted black. Reportedly, it wasn't even a street-legal machine. It's still remembered by hot-rod fans of the period, but there is now the opportunity to actually drive a recreation of the original Hemi Dart.

During those days, certain performance Dodge dealer-

The front view of the Mr. Norm Mopar machine has that huge functional hood scoop with the twin-carb air cleaners visible. Very, very cool!

No mistaking that resto emblem sitting on the rear quarter of the Mr. Norm car.

There are two Hemi engines available for this Mr. Norm creation. The 528-cubic-inch version is capable of 725 horses, but if you want something a little mellower, you can use a smaller 472-cid version with 600 horses.

ships sold the powerful Darts, and the famous Mr. Norm's Grand Spaulding Dodge dealership in Chicago sold more of them than anybody. The idea to build a Resto version of the model was devised by Mr. Norm and Blue Moon Motorsports. It would be a wild and crazy machine, but street-legal in this second lifetime. This would also be an effective drag-race machine and it was soon exercised in that mode with the first example that was built.

Compared to the bare-bones philosophy of the original, the modern Hemi Dart seems luxurious. The original had only <u>one</u> option, that being the choice of an automatic or a manual transmission. Those cars cost a smidge over five grand.

As you might suspect, the recreations require a few more dollars, almost $150,000. Surprisingly, they will have a similarity in that they both use the same body, donor 1968 Dart bodies.

This rear view of the Dodge Dart dragster carries the familiar Mr. Norm GSS circular logo contained within the rear stripes.

But externally is about as far as the similarity exists. There's Hemi power under the hood, but instead of the original 426-cid version, we're talking a brawling 528-cid version, among others, which can put down an awe-inspiring 725-horsepower.

And there is a 426 engine that has been stroked to 472 cubes that provide up to 600 horses. With both engines, buyers can select either an iron or aluminum block.

The power train continues with a four-speed A833 overdrive tranny and a Dana 60 rear end. With those kinds of horses, it's easy to understand that the power-to-weight ratio of this model far exceeds that of the original.

The engine carries a pair of monster four-barrel carbs that are visible from the front of the blackout hood. Is this so cool? But it's certainly not surprising since it has that Mr. Norm association.

And check out the comfort level that you can have when you pull this machine to the line. Included are air conditioning, power steering and brakes, a killer sound system and a number of different trim options.

In an interesting nod to the past, the new Dart comes with both radio and heater delete, just like the original. But unlike the original, those options can be ordered. However, they will be hidden from view so as to give that nostalgic no-frills look. And yes, there is a back seat in the 2000s version and that was not the case with the original!

Initial plans called for about 40 of the model to be produced. As of April 2007, there had been a dozen built. You better believe that these Mr. Norm's Dodge Dart GSS machines are going to be a popular collectable.

A small fleet of Cobra Mark IIIs await their engines at the Dynamics Motorsports Dealership.

SUPERFORMANCE REPLICARS

This company brings a different approach to its replica car business. In its own words: "Superformance manufactures component vehicles for the discerning enthusiast who is looking for a superbly-crafted, factory-built product."

The method of acquisition for these Superformance creations is quite unique. First of all, the cars are manufactured in South Africa and shipped, without engine and transmission, to dealers in the United States. That is the way the cars are purchased. It is then up to the customer to select the engine and tranny to be installed. Finally, a non-affiliated engine shop will make the installation.

Superformance cars are not to be confused with kit cars. They are a complete, ground-up-constructed machine. It's not a body that is laid over an existing chassis to create a new look.

The company explained that the process is similar to the 1960s technique used with the original Ford Cobra. The completed chassis, sans engine and transmission, was mated with the body from AC Cars of England.

There are three classic models that receive the Superformance process: the Mark III Cobra, the Daytona Le Mans Coupe, and the GT40. Here are the hows and whys of these magnificent machines:

Coming at you is the classic AC Cobra straight out of the 1960s, right? No, it's the 2007 Mark III Cobra, a remarkable production by Superformance.

THE MARK III COBRA

This machine is almost an exact copy of the original Cobra, but with the addition of new technology in certain areas, it's much better than the original.

It features modern factory-engineered Bilstein coil-over progressive shocks with custom H&R springs. Four-wheel Wildwood four-piston, caliper-vented power-assisted disc brakes bring this Cobra to a stop quickly and safely. The latest composite glass-fiber technology was used in the body fabrication.

For a little driver creature comfort, the door hinges were raised four inches to clear the driver's shin. Also, the floor was lowered and the compartment widened in order to accommodated taller and larger drivers.

Outside air intake is readily visible on the Mark III. The hood scoop is actually larger than the original to accomplish better engine breathing.

It looks exactly like a Cobra, but it's a magnificent Superformance recreation. Under those classic lines is modern high-tech in terms of brakes, suspension and the engine.

This Superformance Mark III Cobra has it all, from its vertical bumper tips and knock-off wheels to the lake pipes and "paper clip" roll bar.

The hood scoop is enlarged for better engine breathing. Then, a new state-of-the-art Dana Hydralock limited slip differential is fitted as standard equipment. The Tremec five-speed and Ford Top-Loader four-speed transmissions are the choices for this combination. The suspension is high-tech with a four-wheel independent system. Tires are sized at 255/60-15 in the front and 275/60-15 in the rear.

Granted, there is a ton of new technology for this replicar Cobra, but Superformance has also maintained original equipment when it is considered satisfactory to accomplish its duties.

The originality extends to the original Smith Gauges, oil cooler and braided lines. There are numerous other items that are based on the original style, including the aluminum pin-drive knock-off hubs, Moto-Lita wood steering wheel, pedals, catches and fittings, hand brake, side pipes and headers, and stainless-steel fuel tank.

Surprisingly, one of the highest-tech parts of this car is the aluminum-core radiator with two thermostatically controlled electric fans.

The custom-built chassis is fabricated of a parallel ladder frame of heavy wall 2 x 4 inches. With a wheelbase of 90 inches and an overall length of 152 inches, the Superformance Cobra is identical dimensionally with the original.

As a roller, the Mark III weighs 1,840 pounds, with the choice of three engines—the 351, the 427 and the 460. The resulting weights are 2,520, 2,680 and 2,660 pounds, respectively.

Finally, it must be noted that there are two versions of the Mark III. First, there is the Sport with the classic side-mounted exhausts that were built to original specifications. Even ceramic-coated versions are also available. The Mark III Roadster versions carry custom-made mufflers and tailpipes with stainless-steel extensions and head shields.

An important aspect of this model is that it is built under license from Carroll Shelby Licensing Inc. Also, these cars compete in vintage racing, and Superformance Mark IIIs and have won the challenging "One Lap of America" three years in a row.

THE DAYTONA COUPE

Superformance has a unique way of introducing this particular replicar in its brochures. It's enough to make any race-oriented baby boomer's mouth water. It goes something like this:

"What if you had the chance to do it over again, a second chance? Would you do it differently? Could you do it better? Under the pressures of life's deadlines and constraints, we all take shortcuts and wind up with something less than we dreamed. That was certainly the case with racing in the 1960s. Budgets were tight and had to be finished tonight to win tomorrow."

Peter Brock, the designer of the Daytona Coupe; Bob Negstad, designer of the 427 Cobra chassis and suspension; and Bob Olthoff, driver of the winningest coupe of

If anyone missed the Cobra Daytona Coupe in the 1960s, the Superformance Repocar Mark III Cobra coupe offers their version.

The second Superformance Repocar was a direct descendent of the Mark III Cobra, the Daytona Coupe. Like the Mark III, it's filled to the brim with modern innovations.

all time, were given the job of designing a repro version of the classic machine.

Thus, the Daytona Coupe became the second link in the company's classic-car chain. What they achieved was a street-legal repro-car (or Grand Touring Car) capable of transporting two lucky people great distances at high speeds in total comfort. But maybe the greatest enjoyment would be the head-snapping turns from the observers of this magnificent machine.

Quite frankly, it's a combination of the best vintage aspects of the model coupled with current high-tech additions. The frame, for example, is fashioned from tubular steel pieces with an integrated roll bar. The body is built of high-strength composites with carbon-fiber panels.

The suspension is designed by Negstad with unequal-length double wishbones and an anti-roll bar in the front

and rear. The ride is smoothed by modern Bilstein coil-overs with H&R Shocks. The wheels are 18-inch units with real knock-off hubs.

Performance here? You bet. Again, the engine size and builder is the choice of the customer, but testing with a Ford 402-cube engine produced amazing results. The Daytona was able to reach 140 mph in just 15 seconds and it ran a mile with a top speed of 179 mph.

As far as its actual competition in the 1960s, the Daytona was designed as a replacement for the Cobra, which was found to be seriously hurting in the aerodynamics area because of its blunt front shape. So Carroll Shelby called upon Peter Brock to design a new body for the Cobra and the Daytona Coupe was born. With its long sweeping nose, the Daytona solved the problem.

Two resto versions of the famous Ford GT-40 were built in the 2000s. Ford Motor Co. built the GT. And there's this almost perfect restoration of the vehicle with the same dimensions as the original, unlike the 2005-2007 Ford GT.

THE GT-40 MKII A

One of the most recognizable of the 1960s road racing vehicles was the super-slick GT-40 machine that looked like it was reaching supersonic speeds just sitting still. The GT portion of the name came from the Gran Turismo racing, an Italian-named European competition. It's always rated as one of the classic vehicles in that era and it's not surprising that it was selected for recreation by Superformance.

Of course, there was also the Ford Company effort to produce their GT model starting in 2003. That vehicle had the overall look of the GT, but was somewhat larger than the original and used a much greater percentage of modern parts and pieces.

Such is not the case with this model that is so authentic that it can legally use the name of "GT-40."

The recreation of the GT-40 was accomplished with meticulous effort directed toward total originality. In fact, some 90 percent of the vehicle's parts are interchangeable with the original car and chassis. The first production model was completed in May 2005.

Starting with the power train, the Superformance version sports a modern 427-cid, 550-hp engine as compared to the same displacement original engine that produced 485 horses. The new engine's compression ratio of 10.25 was almost identical with the original engine's 10.5 value. It is possible, though, to acquire fuel injection with the modern engine version.

The new GT-40 has a five-speed manual transmission and has a more than 200 mph capability in fifth gear. In the quarter mile, it has demonstrated an 11.2-second, 135 mph capability, which is slightly better than the original.

Inside the recreation, the interior is quite similar to the original including the left-hand drive. It sports original-style seats with the driver's seat three inches wider than the original. In terms of creature comforts, the GT-40 carries air conditioning. Also, the instrument panel is equipped with modern Smith Gauges. There is a so-called

Another modern Roush Crate Engine sits in a Superformance GT-40. Of interest is the exotic and complex exhaust system.

"Gurney Bubble" which allows greater headroom for taller drivers.

The suspension is done pretty much in original trim with the exception of the modern Wilwood "Super Light" brakes. Also, there's an adjustable pedal box, a cross-flow radiator and twin stainless steel baffled fuel tanks mounted in the door sills.

Talk about intakes, they are everywhere on the Superformance GT-40, just like the original. A retro road rocket? You better believe it!

The modern exhausts are configured in the original "Bundle of Snakes" configuration. Modern spoked Halibrand-style wheels are in place. Also, for ease of driving, the shifter and hand brake are located in the center of the tunnel.

Like other Superformance models, this is just about as close to the original as you can get.

XV Motorsports likes to describe its Resto-Mod machines as "A Wolf in Wolf's Clothing." These cars have been designed from the ground up to achieve the highest performance and best handling.

XV MOTORSPORTS

The mission statement of XV Motorsports says the car is: "Designed, engineered, and built from the ground up to strike terror into the hearts of contemporary luxury exotic owners, on the street or on the track. XV Motorsports has taken the concept of a modernized muscle car to a level never before attained using OE and professional motorsports technology unheard of in the performance aftermarket. Nothing else even comes close."

This is what it all means. Using 1960s through '70s muscle-car bodies—the Cuda, Challenger, Charger, Road Runner, GTX and Super Bee—XV builds the ultimate chassis and power train underneath to acquire super performance. The fact that the changes made are pretty much identical is the reason that XV is included in the Continuation Car category.

In the engine department, only the modern 5.7- and 6.1-liter Hemi crate engines are employed. President John Boscemi explained that the XV cars are a complete package with many of the parts and pieces custom-fabricated by XV.

"Our components and systems are truly unique in the industry, having been fully developed, engineered and tested in computer-simulated and real-world environments using state-of-the-art automotive technology."

The only engines used in the XV machines are modern 5.7- and 6.1-liter Hemi versions. Note that the engine bay still has a vintage look with that familiar air cleaner configuration.

Here are some of the vintage Mopar models that have been modified with the XV Motorsports upgrades.

SHELBY CONTINUATION VEHICLES

GT-350SR

The GT-350SR reaches back to the mid-1960s Shelby racing efforts. The standard engine is a modern Shelby-tuned 331-cubic inch, 410-horsepower mauler. The transmission is the very popular Resto-Mod Tremec T5 five-speed manual. Next comes the aluminum driveshaft with a safety loop.

The engine features a Griffen aluminum cross-flow radiator and JBA 2 1/2-inch side exhaust system. The front and rear disc brakes are by Baer. The interior is completely custom with Shelby Signature Gauges, Lecarra wheel, Sony Stereo, 160 mph speedometer, four-point roll bar with horizontal bar, four-point seat belts and an Omega GPS tracking system.

The exterior has R-styled wheels and nose, hood and side scoops. There is a functional SC Cobra-style gas lid with splash bucket, racing side mirrors and an OEM rear glass mirror.

There are numerous options including a 408-cid, 475-horse engine, a TKO five-speed manual tranny, JMC hydraulic clutch, Shelby Hi-Back Bucket Seats, 3-inch-wide seat belts and a trunk-mounted battery.

Power for the GT-350SR comes from a 347-cid, 410-horse fuel-injected engine. The FI system looks amazingly like the original 1960s set-up.
Unique Performance

This GT-350SR definitely has a racing look with that number adorning the door. The lack of the front bumper gives it a sleek look.
Unique Performance

Here's the rear view of the GT-350SR from the rear with a good look at the 1960s-style dual racing stripes. Note that the bumper is painted body color. *Unique Performance*

The 2007 version bears an uncanny resemblance to the 1967 GT-500. The modern version is called the Shelby GT-500E Eleanor. These models are listed in the Shelby American World Registry. Replicas were used in the movie "Gone in 60 Seconds." *Unique Performance*

GT-500SR

It wouldn't be long until a GT-500SR would appear on the scene. The car is carried as a '68 retro model even though almost identical 1967 bodies might be used.

The GT-500SR is bad to the bone with an R-model fiberglass front apron instead of the normal bumper. The expected twin over-body racing stripes are in place and the larger wheels add a new look to that old familiar body.

What engine would be logical for this stunner 'Tang? You got it! A 427 of course—only in this application, it would be a modern aluminum version with D C & O Electronic Fuel Injection. The system carries the look of the vintage, and extremely popular, Weber Carb set-up. And would you believe that there are some 600 ponies rolling out?

The power train continues with a Tremec TKO 500 five-speed manual tranny along with a Currie TruTrack rear end.

But with that type of pounding power to the ground, it was necessary to perform considerable strengthening of the chassis. The suspension is very similar to that used in the GT-500E model. The control arms are Tig-welded pieces, while turning this hauler is accomplished by a rack-and-pinion system.

CSX 4000 Shelby Cobra

The Shelby Cobra was one of the most popular vehicles ever built, as can be affirmed by the multitude of replica kits that have been available for decades. But there has never been anything like these Cobra Resto-Mods.

The CSX 4000 is the modern recreation of the 427 version of the Cobra with the expected modern touch. Although high tech prevails throughout the model, the original frame configuration was retained.

Just looking at the front of the GT-500SR affirms that this is one bad machine. The modern 427 FI engine pounds down over 600 horsepower and is hooked to a Tremec five-speed transmission. *Unique Performance*

The 4000 also features rack and pinion steering, Baer disc brakes with Shelby Calipers and 15-inch Halibrand Pin Drive Wheels.

The bodies are extremely close to the original and can be had in fiberglass, carbon fiber or aluminum. As are all of the Shelby continuation cars, the CSX 4000 versions are documented by Shelby CSX numbers and a manufacturer's statement of origin signed by Carroll Shelby himself.

The customer selects the 427 engine and transmission to be used. With a vehicle equipped with a 427 aluminum Shelby engine, the machine demonstrated 12-second quarter mile performance and a 0-to-60 clocking under four seconds.

CSX 7000/8000 Shelby Cobras

The two Shelby Cobra 289 continuation cars are authentic recreations of the Shelby Cobra 289 models that burned up the international road courses back in the 1960s.

They are component cars that incorporate modern safety and performance improvements without sacrificing driving excitement or originality. The CSX 7000 bodies are available in either fiberglass or aluminum, while the CSX 8000 bodies can be acquired only in fiberglass.

These cars are built for small-block engines of the customer's choice. The Shelby rear end carries Dana 44 gears at a 3.54 ratio. Differences in the cars are that both the painted heavy-duty spoke rims and chrome heavy duty-spoke rims are available with the CSX 8000 model, while an oil-cooler assembly is an option on the CSX 7000.

The rear view of the GT-500SR, in this case a convertible, is a dynamite looker. Note the rear stripes and the correct roll bar. *Unique Performance*

The wheel and brake combination is a thing of beauty and functionality with the Foose five-spoked wheel and the large Baer disc brakes. *Unique Performance*

CHIP FOOSE RESTO-MODS

There is a Unique Performance advertisement that really speaks volumes about the company's building skills. The ad shows a Resto-Mod Shelby Mustang in the background and a dynamite 1969 Chevy Camaro Resto in the foreground. The ad states: "First Make History-Then Repeat It."

The explanation is that not only does Unique Performance build the Shelby continuation cars, but also the designs of Chip Foose. The first was this 1969 Camaro (just like the Baldwin-Motion version) and it is really something else.

The 1969 Foose Camaro is refined with extended rocker panels, a custom front valance and a triangular hood scoop. *Unique Performance*

THE FOOSE '69 CAMARO

The outward appearance is highlighted with an RS-style grille and hood, Jaguar door handles and smoothed bumpers. In addition, there is a custom triangular hood scoop with the front opening containing three horizontal bars, extended rocker panels, a custom front valance, 18-inch five-spoke Foose Wheels, PIAA driving lights and Foose badge identification.

In an interesting touch, these Foose Camaros will be easily identified as they will all be painted the same color scheme, the body in Hugger Orange with a pewter hood and deck lid.

Under the hood, it's the customer's choice of three different engines, actually pretty much from mild to wild. There is the 350-cid, 350-horse ZZ4 GM crate engine. Moving up a performance notch, there's the 6.0-liter LS2 Chevy that is capable of an impressive 390 ponies. The top gun, though, displaces 572 cubes and that buys you a ground-pounding 620 horses. Each of these engines can be purchased with electronic fuel injection.

The Camaro can be equipped with up to a 22-gallon fuel cell. There are also 2.5-inch exhaust pipes and Spintech mufflers. An expected Tremec TKO five-speed is also in place with a Currie 3.25-geared rear end.

Just looking at the macho stance, you know there is some heavy underpinnings doing their job. They consist of tubular

The interior of the Foose Camaro features a Lecarra wheel, custom Auto Meter gauges, a billet shifter and custom black buckets. *Unique Performance*

A-arms, coil-over shocks and a power-steering rack. The rear suspension parrots that of the GT-350SR. For added strength, the front and rear sub-frames are joined together for extra strength.

Stopping this brute quickly comes from the 12-inch discs on each corner with PBR dual-piston calipers.

But what would a Foose Resto machine be without one of his custom interiors? No worry here as that magic Foose touch is also in action. There are classy custom black buckets, lower console and door panels.

Next, there's the billet shifter, a Lecarra steering wheel and silver-faced Auto Meter gauges. The racing touch is in place with a four-point roll cage and five-point seat belts. Sweet sounds come forth from a Sony system, and there is even an optional GPS system.

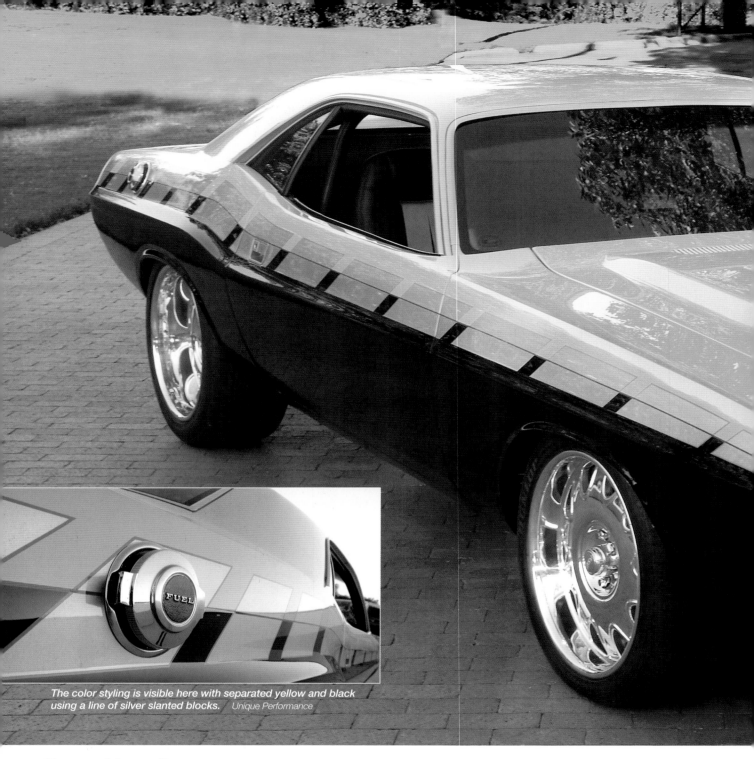

The color styling is visible here with separated yellow and black using a line of silver slanted blocks. Unique Performance

FOOSE HEMI CHALLENGER

Like the Camaro just discussed, an original donor body was used to create this magnificent Foose Hemi Charger that was also assembled by Unique Performance.

The external appearance was startling to say the least. It was a two tone with yellow on the top including the rear deck and hood, and black on the remainder of the car. But it's the dividing line that really sets off the machine. The line consists of a series of slanted silver rectangles that remind one of the vintage AAR 'Cuda stripes.

The base engine is a modern, carbureted 5.7-liter Hemi that gets you about 360 horsepower. If you'd like

a bunch more power for a lot more money ($7,000), you can get it fuel-injected. If you want the ultimate, though, you can order the 426 Hemi crate engine which pumps out an awesome 540 horsepower.

A Tremec TKO five-speed is in place, equipped with a custom hydraulic clutch system hooked to a 31-spline, nine-inch Ford differential with 3.89 gears.

The suspension is totally modern with a rear suspension consisting of laid-down coil-over shocks, while up front there is a K-member with tubular front coil-over suspension.

"Extreme" is certainly the correct name for the Baer

Dodge Challenger was one of the more memorable styles of the muscle car era and it makes sense that there is a Challenger Resto-Mod version by Foose. Unique Performance

Extreme 14-inch front disc brakes and rear 13-inchers with slotted rotors.

With the kind of punch this car's engine has, there needed to be strengthening done to the frame. That was addressed with custom sub-frame connectors. The four-point roll cage is standard equipment.

The interior is business-like with vinyl and suede high-back buckets. The navigation custom console is an electronic masterpiece encompassing a number of features. The steering system is a quick-ratio power-steering rack and adjustable column.

Typical Chip Foose—what more can you say?

This modern 5.7-liter carbureted Hemi engine is the standard power plant for the Foose Challenger. It provides about 360 horsepower. Unique Performance

The YearOne Bandit Trans Am will be produced in numbers using original 1977 through 1979 Pontiac Trans Am bodies. *YearOne*

YearOne Bandit Resto-Mods

Normally, YearOne just produces one-off Resto-Mods to advertise its products. But 2007 being the 30th anniversary of the "Smokey and the Bandit" movie, the company teamed up with star Burt Reynolds to build a limited number of Bandit Resto-Mods using original 1977 through '79 Trans Ams.

The new Bandits will be constructed in three different configurations. The first level (called the Ban1 model) will incorporate flush-mounted front and rear glass, flush fender flairs, LED tail-lights and projector beam headlights. The model also got special Bandit appointments inside.

The suspension was upgraded with tubular upper control arms, high-performance leaf springs and sub-frame connectors. A Pontiac 455-cid, 450-horse engine was hooked to either a five-speed manual or automatic. The ten-bolt rear end carried 3.42 gears.

The trademark of those Bandit machines was the snowflake-style wheels, and the Ban1 carries an updated version of them, only they are 18 inches in diameter.

The so-called Ban2 is more of a performance version with a tubular front sub-frame, front racing-style coil-overs, and bigger brakes.

Horsepower is upped a hundred over the Ban1 model, or a fuel-injected version was also available.

All-out performance is the keynote of the final Ban3 model with a 700-horse pounder under the hood, which can be achieved by either an all-aluminum 455 Pontiac, or an equivalent LS engine. The chassis and suspension are further upgraded to handle the extra horsepower.

At press time, the exact number of Bandits to be produced had not been determined.

Assembly is pretty much a hands-on operation as can be seen from this photo. *YearOne*

CHAPTER 4

GM RESTO-MODS

The total stock look of this classic 1957 Chevy is certainly maintained in this Ohio Resto-Mod.

Unlike the trickle of Resto-Mods using the Ford and Mopar brands, the use of 1950s GM models, especially Chevrolets, is enjoying huge popularity.

In particular, the 1955-1957 Tri-Five models are super popular for the Resto-Mod application. With the availability of the new '57 body from CARS Inc., that style could be continued indefinitely.

Also, the horizontal-finned 1959 Chevrolet has been seen in the Resto-Mod venue. Even 1950s 'Vettes have been utilized to a surprising extent in this mode.

Where it might have been expected that the muscle-car Chevys would be the prime R-Mod versions for the 1960s, that isn't totally the case. Numerous early 1960s models have been noted, with the Impala being a huge favorite.

During the late 1960s, there were two Chevy models that stood out. Certainly, the Camaro was the top model selected, with probably the '69 model year being the biggest contributor.

A close second would have to be the sleek 1966-through-1970 Chevelles. With their macho body styles, this brand really stands tall in the Resto-Mod world. Although it might seem surprising, even the squarish 1960s Chevy IIs and Novas have also found favor with the R-M builders.

In the 1970s, it appears that the Chevelles are the most popular, with Camaros a close second.

Although a vast majority of the General Motors Resto-Mod conversions are Chevy-based, there are also a number of Restos using other brands. Pontiac models have been used, with probably the most numerous being Firebird and Trans-Am models. Their similarity to the Camaros probably helps in their selection. Bigger models such as Catalinas and Grand Prixs have also been seen.

And there are even a few Buicks and Oldsmobiles that have been modified. This chapter will provide coverage of some of the finest General Motors Resto-Mods in the nation. Enjoy!

Owner Gene Flaugher likes the stock look of 1950s Chevys and he kept it that way with this 1954 Resto-Mod conversion.

1954 CHEVY RESTO-MOD

Gene Flaugher bought what was left of this vintage Bowtie vehicle in 2002. "It was rusty and there was no engine or transmission. I had this type of conversion in mind when I bought it, which originally had a six-cylinder power plant," he said.

The suspension set-up is impressive, with a Mustang II front suspension with coil springs and gas shocks. In the rear, aftermarket leaf springs, with two extra leafs, were installed. Also, there are air shocks on the rear.

The modern engine is joined to a modern 41-60E computerized automatic transmission with an Oldsmobile F-85 rear end.

It's a great Resto-Mod build-up effort done by Flaugher at an economical price tag.

Builder and owner: Gene Flaugher

The custom instrument panel carries VDO white-face units. The seats and door panels are done meticulously in red vinyl. The steering wheel is by Grant.

This is a 2003 5.3-liter Silverado truck engine capable of 275 horsepower. It features body-colored engine covers matching the engine compartment.

"Plush" would have to be the descripton of this Chevy Resto-Mod interior. The same beige color is carried throughout. Wickett

1955 Chevy 210 Resto-Mod

Using the base 1955 210 body style makes the appearance of this Resto-Mod somewhat unique. The machine is powered by a modern 454-cid engine that is detailed in the body color. It's hooked to a 700R4 transmission. There's Corvette suspension front and rear with 'Vette coil-over shocks on the front plus Corvette leaf springs on the rear.

The chassis is by California Chassis, which was modified by Hot Rod Construction. Boyd Coddington wheels are in place with 17-inch front and 18-inch rear tires. The interior is totally customized, with a Victory Red base-coat, clear-coat. Awards include Top-25 in "Shades of the Past," a Boyd Coddington Pro Pick, seven Good Guy awards in 2004 and a Super Chevy Best-of-Show.

Builder: Hot Rod Construction
Owner: Jack Jenkins

The distinctive Boyd Coddington wheels are the only portion of the car that aren't stock. They are 17 inches in the front and 18 inches in the rear. *Wickett*

This magnificent engine is almost devoid of wires and other accessories. Carrying the body color, you swear that you could eat off of the engine's surface. *Wickett*

This 1955 Chevy Resto-Mod might fool you with its basic body style, but closer examination will surprise you. *Wickett*

1955 CHEVY BEL AIR RESTO-MOD

This classy 1950s red and white Resto-Mod has excellence everywhere you look. That modern all-chrome 355-cid, 9.0:1 compression Edelbrock engine has a Mallory Ignition, Street & Performance block headers and a Flowmaster exhaust. It also has Wilwood front disc brakes, Heidts tubular A-arms, air ride, Shock Wave shocks and custom five-spoke wheels.

The custom interior features a Billet Specialties tilt wheel, custom console, aluminum trim, power seats, Dakota Digital Instruments, with all power switches hidden. Modifications include hand-fabricated inner fenders, radiator cover and core.

Builder: Danny Wickett
Owner: Hasty's Car Country

The center console of this one-off Resto-Mod extends forward into the transmission hump. The all-digital instruments provide data in blue.

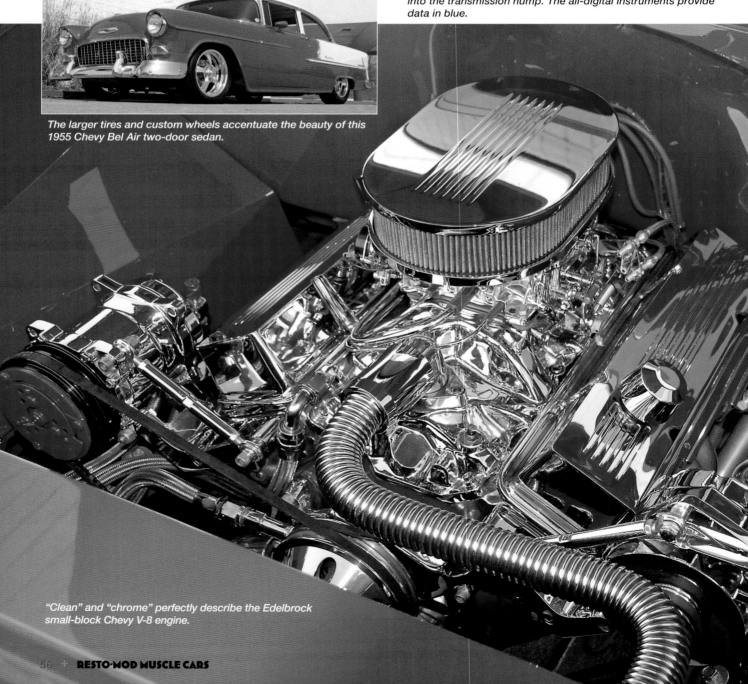

The larger tires and custom wheels accentuate the beauty of this 1955 Chevy Bel Air two-door sedan.

"Clean" and "chrome" perfectly describe the Edelbrock small-block Chevy V-8 engine.

Modern fabrication technology has been applied but the 1955 Chevy mystique still is in evidence. The rear license plate has been recessed and the gas door and the trunk are remotely operated.

The custom interior contains all the bells and whistles including a Corvette steering column, owner-built steering wheel, modern Moon Gauges, hidden glove box, custom seats and more!

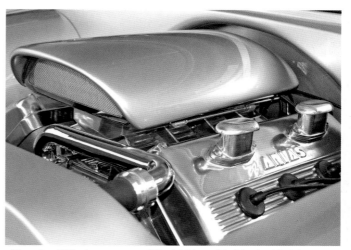

There's a 700+ horsepower 468-cid Chevy big block with Arias Hemi heads and 10-1 Hemi pistons, plus Manley Rods and a forged crank. The owner-built air cleaner uses the same curvature as the 1955 Chevy fenders covering the headlights.

1955 CHEVY RESTO-MOD

Brian Baker has owned his 1955 Chevy since the 1970s, but it has certainly never looked like this during those early years. These days, it has one of the best looks of any Resto-Mod. The body has been cleaned and smoothed to ultimate perfection, but not to the point of departing from its 1955 Chevy heritage.

Next, there's that dynamite power train consisting of a monster Arias-headed engine attached to a B&M-modified TH400 transmission and an advanced rear end with a Winters aluminum center section and a nine-inch Detroit Locker.

It rides as good as it looks with a custom fabricated frame with 3 x 5-inch frame rails, stainless steel brake lines, tubular removable transmission cross member, and a four bar rear housing with coil-over suspension.

It's top drawer in every aspect!

Builder: Bakers Vintage Automotive Inc.
Owner: Brian Baker

This classic 1955 Chevy just knocks you out with its Vintage Platinum color. Except for its rear fender chrome, the body has been completely smoothed. The Billet Specialties wheels finish the Resto-Mod fantasy.

1956 CHEVY RESTO-MOD

Guess it's not hard to understand why this 40th anniversary Resto-Mod was in the opening scene of the movie, "The Boulder Shoot-Out." It has also won numerous national awards. Meticulous preparation was accomplished to produce the superb finish on this body.

Every aspect of this vintage Bowtie is of the highest detail. The car drives as well as it looks with a modern high-tech suspension system, consisting of a PSI front sway bar and bushings, Monroe Sensi-Track gas shocks, and dropped front spindles.

Builder: California Customs
Owner: John Scherer

The interior is done in a gray tweed and dove gray leather. The dash is mostly stock with VDO gauges. *John Scherer*

It looks as good underneath as it does from above. The '56 Chevy features a ceramic-coated exhaust system, stainless steel gas tank and a polished differential. *John Scherer*

The GM 502 crate engine offers 440 horsepower. It's hooked to a 700 R4 four-speed automatic transmission with a TCI Torque converter.
John Scherer

This 1956 Chevy 210 two-door hardtop carries an almost stock look. One hint to its Resto-Mod status are the custom five-spoke wheels.
John Scherer

1957 CHEVY BEL AIR RESTO-MOD

Normally, a modern-engined Resto-Mod is thought of as a performance car. That's certainly true with this '57 Chevy Bel Air, and its modern LS-1 5.7-liter aluminum V-8. It gets well over 20 miles per gallon. Owner Calvin Fleek explained, "It drives like a dream, and with modern four-wheel disc brakes, it stops right now."

And this silver beauty really gets the attention when it arrives at a car show or cruise-in. Even though it's a classic model that has been modified in this manner, there is certainly no objection to the perfection that has evolved.

Builder: Jim Humbert
Owner: Calvin Fleek

One of the most popular cars from the 1950s is the 1957 Chevy. This two-door hardtop version has been preserved in Resto-Mod form.

The engine is a modern Corvette aluminum LS-1 version with stock GM parts. Note that the engine compartment carries the external body color.

The interior is done in gray leather with beige inserts. The steering column and pedals are by Heidts. Also, there's a vintage air-conditioner unit under the dash.

1965 Chevelle Resto-Mod

Granted, this Resto is a four-door, but the way it sits, you just forget about the supposed "family look."

High tech is in place for the suspension system with tubular upper and lower control arms by Global West both front and rear. Also, there are QA-1 aluminum adjustable shocks on all four corners, a pair of beefy sway bars and all polyurethane bushings.

Power comes from a modified 2000 Vette LT-1 engine that is pushing big horsepower numbers. The tranny is also of the modern nature with a 1999 4L60E unit and a GM 10 bolt with an Eaton "Trac Lock" differential.

Braking is accomplished with modern Baer Disc Brakes with 13-inch slotted discs and aluminum calipers. They bring to a halt Billet Specialties "Roulette" wheels with powder-coated accents.

Even with all the changes made to the remainder of the machine, the frame was retained in basically stock trim with just a few minor changes made for fitting of the new parts.

Builder: Ultimate Customs
Owner: Jim O'Conell

It's called the "White Bomb" and this 1965 Chevelle Resto-Mod certainly fills the bill. The body has all its original panels and is beautifully finished in 2006 Corvette Arctic White base coat with clear coat. *Douglas Sonders*

The custom interior is highlighted with red leather, remolded factory seats and a Billet Specialties steering wheel.
Douglas Sonders

The engine is from the modern era—a 2000 Corvette LS-1 power plant equipped with a number of aftermarket performance parts.
Douglas Sonders

1967 Chevelle Resto-Mod

It's all business just sitting there with a look that is certainly a one-of-a-kind Bowtie Resto-Mod. With that low-slung stance and sinister cold black paint scheme, it certainly gets your attention in a big way.

The model uses a gloriously detailed and powerfully injected LS-5 Corvette engine with twin turbo-chargers. Other goodies include a Corvette C4 suspension system with air ride and Baer 13-inch disc brakes on all four corners. The custom chassis was built by Hot Rod Construction (HRC).

The engine compartment was hand-formed, while HRC fabricated the custom hood, grille, drip moldings, dash, console and tail lights. The classy interior is done in leather. There's even a rear-view video camera.

Competition awards include a first at the 2006 Detroit Autorama, YearOne Cup Winner and first in the Good Guys Southeaster Nationals.

Builder: Hot Rod Construction

Performance and appearance are under the hood with a twin-turbocharged and injected LS-5 Corvette engine. The appearance is beyond words with all the airflow hardware done in chrome. Hot Rod Construction

The body on this 1967 Resto-Mod has been smoothed to perfection giving it the look of a much-newer design. Chrome and door handles have been removed giving it a sleek, clean appearance.   *Hot Rod Construction*

The model carries custom bumpers, both front and rear, along with roll pans.   *Hot Rod Construction*

The trunk is highly detailed in black and gray. It contains embedded, center-facing speakers.   *Hot Rod Construction*

This view shows the rear axle assembly. Note the universals that are just outside the rear end.   *Hot Rod Construction*

1970 Chevy Chevelle Resto-Mod

Although this 1970 Chevelle Resto-Mod might look almost totally stock on the exterior, that's certainly not the case with its performance-personified power plant. That's a 502 horsepower crate engine sitting out front with Flowmaster exhausts and hooked to an R700 tranny and a 12-bolt 3.73 Positraction rear end. Owner Jim Hasty explained that these popular models don't need any enhancement on the outside. The oversized Bridgestone tires are supported by American Racing Torque-Thrust wheels. The interior produces sweet sounds from a modern MDX radio.

Owner: Jim Hasty

The 1970 Chevelle Super Sport was one of the most popular two-door hardtops of the day and its fine lines are preserved in this Resto-Mod version.

That's 502 cubic inches of big block displacement punching out the same number of horsepower from this GM crate engine.

1970 Chevelle SS Convertible Resto-Mod

One of the highlights of this 1970 Chevelle convertible is the body. There was great attention paid to fitting all gaps and body lines. It was painted in black base-coat, clear coat and was polished to a mirror-like finish.

Suspension is high tech with Global West tubular front control arms, Currie trailing arms, an HD front and rear sway bars plus QA1 aluminum adjustable coil-over shocks and powder-coated springs.

The power train is top drawer with a GM 502 Ram Jet Fuel injected crate engine with 502 horses and 570 foot-pounds of torque. The powerhouse is connected to a Richmond five-speed manual tranny with a Currie 12-bolt Positraction with a 3.73 ring and pinion. The power is funneled through Billet Specialty wheels—with 17-inchers in front and size 18 on the rear.

Stopping comes quickly from Wilwood four-wheel disc brakes controlled by a Heidts adjustable proportioning brake valve.

The interior has a modern flair, but maintains much of its original look. White leather covers the interior including the seats and door panels. In addition, there is an Impala factory center console, a modern tilt steering column with a teak wheel, a Viper alarm system and an AM/FM CD custom sound system.

Builder: Custom Classics Inc.

Besides being nicely detailed, the 502-cid engine has the same horsepower figure. It carries a Deep Sump aluminum oil pan, a Billet aluminum March Pulley System and Hooker Headers.
Custom Classics

The external appearance of this 1970 Chevelle convertible Resto-Mod jumps out and grabs you. Those flashy hood stripes and the 17- and 18-inch Billet Specialties wheels and lowered stance are something else! Custom Classics

1969 CAMARO SS RESTO-MOD

The history of this magnificent 1969 Chevy Resto-Mod is interesting, to say the least. Granted, there are a number of aftermarket aspects to the car, but the most interesting is the body itself. In this case, it's a reproduction body.

Builder YearOne decided to see if this type of body could be used to construct a high-end Resto-Mod. There was even a brochure published on the construction process. It was appropriately called "Mail Order Camaro."

It can be done and you can see the results here of one fine Bowtie Resto-Mod.

Builder and owner: YearOne

The custom interior carries a number of YearOne items including the door panels and leather-covered hound's-tooth inserts. The steering wheel is by Flaming River and Grant did the custom wheel. YearOne

The Yenko Camaro Resto-Mod's engine is a modern fuel-injected Ram Air 454 V-8. Fesler Built

1969 CHEVY YENKO CAMARO CLONE RESTO-MOD

Fester Built really has it all together with the building of this Yenko clone Resto-Mod. Granted, it's got all the authentic-style Yenko graphics, and it's based on a '69 Camaro, but that's about where the similarity ends.

This is through-and-through an authentic Resto-Mod with a modern-style power train, suspension system with an air ride, 20-inch wheels and a modern interior to kill for.

Just take a look and salivate.

Builder: Fesler Built

The macho stance adopted by this Resto-Mod was accomplished by adjusting the multi-leaf springs and staggered KYB shocks in the rear and two-inch drop spindles and Eaton Detroit springs in the front. *YearOne*

This striking 1969 Yenko Camaro Resto-Mod carries a correct color and the Yenko striping. *Fesler Built*

1969 Camaro Convertible Resto-Mod

It seems that Hugger Orange is almost spoken in the same sentence with 1969 Camaro. That connection obviously comes from its association with the Indy Pace Car honor that model year.

No doubt about it, that Du Pont Hugger Orange base color combined with the flashy white Z-28 stripes really gets you.

It looks like speed just sitting there. This Camaro can back it up with a power train consisting of a pumped-up 1996 LT-1 with knock-out looks along with a Rick Armstrong 200R4 four-speed and a 1994 LT-1 Positraction unit.

The advanced suspension system features modern dropped spindles along with Rancho bushings and parts. Then, Aero Tech provided the Billet Aluminum Calipers and directional-drilled rotors.

Builder: Red Line Auto Sports
Owner: Fred and Kim Murfin

The interior stayed pretty much in the factory vein with the stock White hound's-tooth and black, along with a vintage air conditioner and a Rosewood steering wheel. Jefferson Bryant

By now, you probably know the '69 Camaro is a hugely popular candidate for Resto-Mods. This rendition features the Z-28 version with its popular Hugger Orange paint. Jefferson Bryant

A 1996 LT-1 engine is custom painted to match the external color and carries aftermarket performance parts. Jefferson Bryant

1969 CHEVY Z-28 CAMARO RESTO-MOD

You gotta love the subtle Resto-Mod of Matt Day. First of all, the classic Glacier Blue base coat detailed with black stripes didn't come from some paint shop. Those are the factory colors.

But raise the hood, and things deviate quickly from stock with a killer 502-cid, 502-horsepower GM crate engine that has been stepped up with a roller tappet cam and intake. That magic HP number is carried on the air cleaner and on the hood. The five-speed Tremec tranny has become the standard for these machines, while there's a 12-bolt Positraction 4.10 rear end out back.

The suspension has been upgraded with traction bars and modern shocks. In order to handle those heavy horses, the factory frame was beefed up with reinforcing.

Eighteen-inch American Racing Torque Thrust wheels really set off this machine, actually giving it different proportions. Day explained that they were custom fitted to the car with the backspacing adjusted for a perfect stance.

The interior is basically stock with the exception of the Pro-Comp Ultralight Gauges. "A lot of people love this interior, including me, and I just didn't think it needed to be changed," Day explained.

Builder and owner: Matt Day

This 1969 Z-28 Camaro Resto-Mod sports its factory Glacier Blue and Black paint scheme. It also rides on its stock frame that has been tied for extra reinforcement and strength.

The rear view of the 1969 Z-28 Camaro Resto-Mod sports a traction bar suspension and modern shocks to align and handle all the power from the modern engine.

It's not factory—Chevy didn't make a 502 in 1969—but understand this GM crate engine has the same number of horses as its cubic-inch displacement.

1969 CAMARO SUPER STOCK RESTO-MOD

Another nifty YearOne creation is this 1969 Camaro Super Stock Resto-Mod. The white and orange machine carries a very stock look except for a custom hood configuration.

The interior is striking with custom front buckets, center console, steering column and cruise control sourced from a 1998 Camaro. Giving it a vintage look are the custom leather covers with the orange and black hound's-tooth inserts that were so popular during the day.

Suspension is high-tech with a Martz front sub-frame with rack-and-pinion steering and an Air Ride Technologies system implemented with tubular control arms. SSBC provided the disc brakes.

The power train is impressive with a modern 4L60E automatic overdrive transmission and a Moser 12-bolt rear end.

Builder: YearOne
Owner: Kevin King

Each wheel well features a beautiful treatment with a Billet Specialties five-spoke design and a Baer disc-brake system.   YearOne

This YearOne 1969 Camaro Resto-Mod was built in the early 2000s and includes advanced fabrication technology.   YearOne

This low rear angle of the YearOne'69 Camaro Resto-Mod really shows off the car's lines, wheels, spoiler and paint job. Anyone care to go for a ride? *YearOne*

The nicely detailed engine is an electronic, fuel-injected LS2 with a Magnuson "Magna Charger" supercharger system. *YearOne*

1973 Z-28 Camaro Resto-Mod

It's nice to report that sometimes the owner of a classic Resto-Mod was responsible for a majority of its construction. Such was the case for Jason Wyrick and his 1973 Camaro. The near-stock body was covered with silver plus black center-body stripes. The modern 383-cid built-up engine is connected to a TKO600 Tremec five-speed hooked to a nine-inch rear end. Suspension is high tech with tubular A-arms, QA-1 coil-over shocks and a mini-four link system in the rear. Brakes are stout for this Camaro with Baer 14-inch two-piece rotors.

Builder and owner: Jason Wyrick

The engine is a modern, built-up 10:1 compression 383-cid engine with Wiseco Pistons, a Holley Stealth Ram EFI System and a hydraulic cam.

The partially custom interior shows Scat Procar seats, white-face Auto Meter gauges, a Lecarra steering wheel and a Classic Industries dash.

The 20-inch tires in the rear give the Resto-Mod version of the '73 Camaro a forward body rake. The dramatic spoked wheels are American Racing Torque Thrust IIs.

The 1973 Camaro was one of the last of the muscle-era cars to retain its muscular lines. This Resto-Mod enhances the original look with a custom front spoiler and a reverse-air hood intake.

1979 Camaro Resto-Mod

In the world of Resto-Mods, this example might be considered too new by many for such a conversion. But the results might convince some to consider this model.

The restoration effort stretched over three years for owner Jeannine Roll. She walked along the production line while the car was being built in Norwood, Ohio.

With a 290 horse Chevy crate engine, it isn't as powerful as some Camaro Restos, but it gets down the road quite nicely, thank you. The remainder of the power train is a reworked 400Turbo automatic and a 3.73 Positraction rear end.

That classy interior is as good as it gets and still carries the factory gauges because the builder liked the way they looked. The suspension is high-tech with an Air Ride system, while stopping is accomplished by four-wheel 11-inch disc brakes.

Not only is this Resto-Mod different in nature, it also stands at or near the top in fabrication excellence.

Builder: Rod Prather
Owner: Jeannine Roll

It has a striking color combination of GM Code 29 Silver and a blue-green color that really sets off this '79 Camaro Resto-Mod. The wheels are Beryen chrome multi-spoke units supporting 19- and 20-inch Kumho tires.

The interior is mostly stock but is covered in two-tone leather. The door panels and the steering wheel are custom items.

"This car (a 1961 Chevy Impala Super Sport Coupe) was built to look as stock as possible but still have the new ride, performance, and handling," the builder indicated. Except for the wheels, it sure does have that stock external look. *Fesler Built*

The 1961 Chevy Impala interior has an all-new look with a two-tone red and white leather motif done by 1st Upholstery. *Fesler Built*

1961 CHEVY IMPALA SS RESTO-MOD

The 1961 Impala Super Sport model has been a popular choice for Resto-Mod creations. This Fesler Built example is one of the best. It might have a deceptive factory look about it, but it's Resto through and through.

The power harks back to a derivation of the original engines for these cars. It's a modern build-up of a 348-cid six-pack Chevy V-8 engine carrying an MSD Ignition and a Flowmaster exhaust system, but it also was built to have a stock look about it. The tranny is a modern four-speed Muncie unit. The ride is smooth with a modern Hotchkiss suspension.

Besides the custom red and white leather upholstery, there are such additions as aftermarket Auto Meter gauges, a Sony CD player hidden in the glove box and a Kicker sound system.

It might look stock on the outside, but that's sure not the case!

Builder: Fesler Built

Budnik (the wheels), Baer (brake power) and Dunlop (the rolling rubber) make a great combination for this 1961 Chevy Impala Resto-Mod. Fesler Built

This engine is a full-built 348 Chevy "six-pack" (three two-barrel carbs) engine. In its day, it was a terror on the drag strips. It's not shy in this format either! Fesler Built

The famed large factory "bubble top" rear window plays sweetly with the Emerald Bliss color scheme of the top of the vintage 1962 Chevy Bel Air Sport Coupe. *Joe Greeves*

Power is aplenty from a GM 572-cubic-inch crate engine. It's been heavily modified and provides more than 600 horsepower. The engine compartment is done in satin with a custom body-color air cleaner cover. *Joe Greeves*

Owner Ken Sarbu started with a great project car and moved to the magnificent version shown here. The body is coated to perfection in Du Pont Hot Hues Emerald Bliss while the bottom carries Du Pont Blacken Black. *Joe Greeves*

1962 CHEVY BEL AIR RESTO-MOD

When Ken Sarbu first bought this 1962 Bel Air, his plans for the machine weren't that ambitious, just a driver-primered rod. But what has evolved is a Resto-Mod of great proportions.

It's done in Du Pont Hot Hues Emerald Bliss and black, and the color scheme is also carried through the interior and engine compartment.

It rides on a GM X-frame and is supported by an Air Ride Technologies suspension system. The giant 20-inch Billet Specialties wheels neatly tuck inside the wheel wells giving the vehicle a slight forward rake.

Hidden behind the chrome, green and black engine compartment is a giant 620-horse, 572-cid Chevy crate engine hooked to a 700R4 four-speed automatic transmission with a B&M 2200 rpm torque converter. The final power train part is a nine-inch Ford rear end.

The interior is striking with custom green buckets and black inserts. The custom black dash carries aftermarket gauges. There is just too much to list in this magnificent Bowtie. One-of-a-kind?? You better believe it!

Builder: Blewetts Rod Shop
Owner: Ken Sarbu

The external colors are a vital part of the interior look. The custom console carries a Lokar Shifter and Classic Industries Tach. The glove compartment was relocated to the center of the dash and the modern gauges were modified to look like the originals. Joe Greeves

A lower angle of the 1962 Chevy Impala SS two-door hardtop Resto-Mod shows off some of its special characteristics, including its low stance.

The 383-cubic-inch "stroker" engine gives this Resto-Mod a big punch of performance with its 500 horses. The chrome-detailed engine carries a 750cfm carburetor.

1962 CHEVY IMPALA SUPER SPORT RESTO-MOD

It was Grandma's proud possession that she bought new. It only has about 38,000 actual miles on it. But since Brian Leach got a hold of it, it would never be recognized.

The power train has been pumped up with a built 383 Stroker Engine that is turning out about 500 horses. In the trunk, there's an extra 250-hp boost when needed from a nitrous system. Next down the line is a modern 700R overdrive tranny and a Currie nine-inch 4.11 Detroit Locker rear end. It's never been put on the drag strip, probably never will be, but the owner figures it's probably a 12-second machine.

The chassis is pretty much stock with an air-ride suspension and tubular control arms. An interesting deviation for this all-out machine is the interior. It's in pretty much stock trim.

"I think the factory interior looks just great, and I haven't found a custom interior to compare," Leach said.

What really knocks you out is that Lexus Absolute Red paint scheme that caresses those fine vintage lines to perfection and also reaches the interior.

Owner: Brian Leach

It takes twin batteries to power this machine. Also in the trunk are both the NOS and Air Ride systems and the booming stereo. There's no room for luggage in this trunk!

The 18-inch front tires seem to add a better proportion to the overall car design than the 14-inchers that originally came with the car.

1963 CHEVY IMPALA RESTO-MOD

It's a dramatic Candy Apple Red in color and that "Impala" name stares at you in ghost letters from the rear quarters.

Owned by Scott Dallis, the vintage Impala was bought new by Scott's wife's aunt. "I bought it for $100 and thought that it would make an excellent Resto-Mod," he said.

You have to look closely to observe the "Impala" lettering that is ghosted on both rear quarters.

Hot flames are licking across the body of this 1963 Impala convertible Resto-Mod. It's already a red-hot machine!

The engine compartment contains a 350-cid, 290-horse GM crate engine that blinds you when the hood is opened. It is completely covered in chrome. The body color is also used to complete the engine mirage, along with covering the undercarriage.

The interior is completely custom, done in tan leather with the carpet in German wool. Surprisingly, the dash was left in factory trim. "Just liked the way it looked and didn't change it," Dallis explained.

Guess it's not surprising to learn that it was rated as one of the top 20 cars in the nation for 2007.

Builder: Jimmy Bonotts
Owner: Scott Dallis

The modern and plush Impala convertible Resto-Mod interior is done completely in leather with a custom console that runs the length of the passenger compartment.

The lift capability of this Resto-Mod is shown. It can sit at its original stock height or at the low-rider position shown here.

Although this is a GM 350 crate engine, you would never guess as it's been chromed. The remainder of the engine compartment is meticulously detailed in the exterior body color.

1964 CHEVY BISCAYNE RESTO-MOD

Wesley Crum has to be proud of his 1964 Chevrolet Biscayne Resto-Mod. It's definitely top-drawer. "I got the car in 1998. It belonged to a neighbor and I played in it when I was a kid," he explained.

Interestingly, the Biscayne was a lower trim level when it was released, but that was then, this is now!

The excellence starts under the hood with a Jack Cunningham-built LS-1 350-cid power plant. Crum places the horsepower in the 390-horse range. It's been detailed to the hilt with flashy engine covers. Then, there's that killer PPG Ruby Anniversary Red body coating which is continued on the undercarriage and interior.

There's an X-frame by Currier that is combined with a tubular Air Technologies A-arm suspension. The interior continues the theme of excellence that was accomplished by Portage Trim and Upholstery.

The body has been smoothed to perfection, but the owner explained that it's still totally stock. It's set off beautifully with those Boyd Coddington wheels.

Builder: Owner and Jack Cunningham
Owner: Wesley Crum

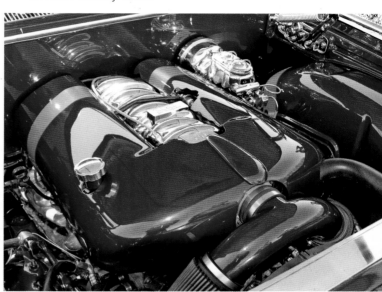

This 1964 Chevy Biscayne Resto-Mod started life as a stripped down model. Now it looks better than any of the fancier Impalas and Impala Super Sport models of that year.

The striking engine compartment carries the metal-flake body color along with considerable chrome detailing. The LS-1 engine sits beneath the custom-built engine cover.

The interior is a custom at the highest level, done in the body color and white. Everything is knock-out modern including the digital dash, Coddington steering wheel and the seats.

1966 Chevy II Nova Resto-Mod

Jerry Montgomery has had this 1966 Nova since 1998, but rest assured that it didn't look like this when he made the purchase. What you see here was done mostly by the owner. Check the ultimate smoothing of the stock body that is now covered by luxurious Torch Red. Also, the looks continue to the engine compartment where it's detailed to the hilt.

The power train consists of a 350 GM crate engine which hooks its 350 ponies to a 700R4 GM four-speed tranny and a Moser 12-bolt rear end. Eleven-inch Wilwood disc brakes on all four corners get this scarlet beauty stopped almost instantly.

Suspension is also high-tech with a Martz Chassis with coil-over shocks, tubular A-arms and sub-frame connectors.

Builder: Jerry Montgomery
Owners: Jerry and Brenda Montgomery

The initial Novas were built to be economy cars, but that sure isn't the case here. It's definitely got a performance look with that low slouch and those 17-inch Budnik spoked wheels.

The Torch Red color of this 1966 Chevy II Nova is evident in just about every aspect of this Resto-Mod version. Undercarriage parts are visible and also carry the volatile exterior shade.

The striking engine compartment sports a body-colored firewall, fender wells and engine cover. The engine is a 350-cid injected GM crate engine that provides 350 horsepower.

1957 CORVETTE RESTO-MOD

The builder of this machine, Yenko Wildfire, likes to call this creation "…an F-16 with a License Plate…" and the title is very appropriate. This particular model had been taken out of storage after 38 years! One of the nice body touches are 3.1/2-inch reinforced rear fender flares.

Right off the bat, the 'Vette was fitted with a top-gun Art Morrison chassis. There is also a C5 suspension system with oversize Wilwood Brakes.

The killer 505-horse LS7 engine is supported by a solid Tremec TKO five-speed transmission and a Strange Engineering rear end.

The interior is totally custom highlighted with ostrich-leather seats. Over $15,000 was spent on chroming, polishing and powder coating. The vehicle also incorporates a GPS, DVD player, air conditioning, electric/hydraulic doors and hood and more.

The visual attraction of the Resto-Mod, though, comes from the artistic flames which invade the car. They are on the body in various locations and light up the engine valve covers. All of the paint and body work was performed by Bobby Wiles and Chad Woodard.

The company indicated that 3,300 hours were expended in the build with some $325,000 invested.

Builders and owners: Yenko Wildfire, headed by Archie Carlini

Check out this engine! Right off the bat, there are those flames licking off the custom valve covers! The LS-7 crate engine is capable of 505 horses, one of only 143 new LS-7 engines built for non-assembly use.
Yenko-Wildfire

Although it certainly doesn't appear to be the case with all the wild, blazing-fire graphics, this car started off as a stock 1957 Corvette body.
Yenko-Wildfire

The flames can be seen from the rear view. It's a one-of-a-kind look!   Yenko-Wildfire

The flames on this dramatic 1957 'Vette Resto-Mod are carried onto the custom dash that also sports seven aftermarket gauges. The seats are done in Ostrich leather.   Yenko-Wildfire

1960 Corvette Resto-Mod

With their unique styling and accessories, one wouldn't think that a vintage Corvette would be a candidate for a Resto-Mod conversion. But that's not the case as there are an increasing number of them being built.

Check out this great-looking example of a 1960 Corvette. Even the purists love this Resto 'Vette. The detailing was done throughout with a custom powder-coated frame. Handling was greatly improved with a modern C4 Corvette suspension.

The power train is potent and modern with a Corvette LS2 crate engine mated to a six-speed manual transmission and concluded with a 3.73 differential. That engine was detailed with body color covers bearing the "Corvette LS2" logo.

The already stylish interior was completely redone with an Ostrich Ultra-Leather covering along with modern seats and convertible top. Classic Instruments provided the custom chrome gauges.

Builder: Corvette Correction Speed shop
Owner: Allen and Lou Ann Nichols

Hidden within this stock-appearing 1960 Corvette are a significant number of modifications that make this a top-drawer Resto-Mod.
Allen Nichols

Smoothie II Coddington wheels support Kumho low-profile wheels on all four corners.   *Allen Nichols*

The custom seats are done in Ostrich Ultra-Leather. Check out that nifty custom console!   Allen Nichols

1987 Monte Carlo SS Aerocoupe Resto-Mod

Builder Bill Rea had been looking for the right 1987 Monte Carlo to perform the ultimate Resto-Mod. He bought the car in 1998. Even though the model is newer than most of the Resto-Mods, the results were outstanding.

The power train for the cold, black machine consists of a modern LS1 engine hooked to a Tremec six-speed tranny and a Curry differential with NASCAR 31-spline axles. The tires are supported by 15-inch Weld Telstar wheels and stopped with Baer disc brakes.

The interior is certainly a looker, highlighted by the custom Wildfire aluminum dashboard that is filled with 11 modern Auto Meter gauges. Then, there's that nifty Momo carbon-fiber steering wheel and hand-stitched leather seats with SS logos.

The chassis is strengthened with Hotchkiss sub-frame connectors. The suspension features Heller 6050 springs, Koni 50/50 shocks and Hotchkiss sway bars.

Builder and owner: Bill Rea

It's a Resto-Mod but a 1980s Resto is a little newer than you would expect. With those 15-inch Telstar Wheels on all four corners, it's got the Resto look. About the only body change is the addition of a Penske-Wallace spoiler.

This has to be the most instrumented dashboard in history! It will take some driver leaning to the right to read those 11 Auto Meter gauges! And there is a Hurst Competition Plus Shifter, Vintage air conditioner and a Panasonic sound system.

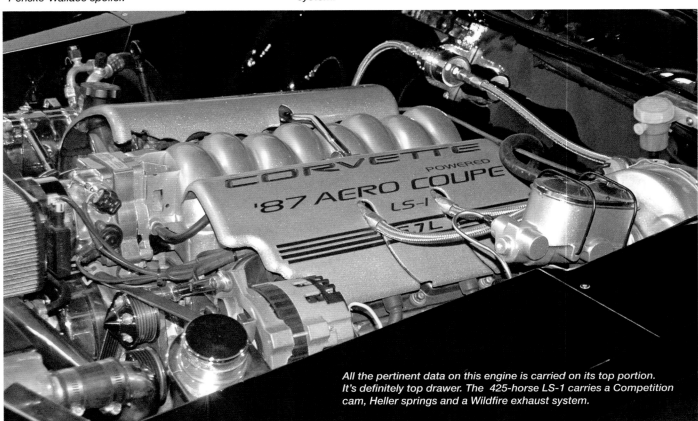

All the pertinent data on this engine is carried on its top portion. It's definitely top drawer. The 425-horse LS-1 carries a Competition cam, Heller springs and a Wildfire exhaust system.

1959 PONTIAC CATALINA RESTO-MOD

Larry Lightcap had a 1959 Pontiac Catalina after he got out of high school, so it's not surprising that he used the same model for his Resto-Mod candidate.

It's the sound of that Pontiac engine that really gets folks grooving. It is a 358-cubic inch Gibbs NASCAR engine with 550 ponies available. It's hooked to a Muncie four-speed and a Pontiac Positraction rear end.

And then there's that striking, upgraded interior that was done in a silver and body-red vinyl. Lightcap built the nifty five-spoke wheels himself.

It's a magnificent and innovative Resto-Mod that blows everybody away, bowing to its sight and sound.

Builder and owner: Larry Lightcap

This engine is definitely a Resto-Mod rarity being an actual 2000 Joe Gibbs Racing NASCAR V-8. The 358-cubic inch power plant produces 550 horsepower.

Among the highlights of this Pontiac Resto-Mod are the dazzling five-spoke wheels. No factory name on this hub because the owner fabricated them himself!

You might not expect to use a 1959 Pontiac Catalina as a Resto-Mod, but this example really makes the grade. The only deviation from stock on the body is the elevated scoop for engine clearance and the rear air entrance.

1965 Pontiac GTO Resto-Mod

"Return of the Great One" was the way the Performance West Group describes its "restofication" of this 1965 GTO. In stock trim, this model was about as macho as it could get, but with this modification, the bar was raised considerably.

Every nook and cranny was smoothed and refined to the modern age. Take the power train and the upgraded 421 Pontiac engine. With its Tri-Power set-up, the engine also sports Cal Custom valve covers.

The modern Muncie M20 four-speed tranny is mated to a Gear Venders Overdrive unit and it is hooked to a GM 12-bolt rear end with a Mr. Gasket finned differential cover.

Hotchkiss Performance was responsible for the chassis with advanced control arms, front and rear coil springs, the boxed rear lower control arms and the rear trailing arms. The SSBC brakes feature 14- and 10.1/2-inch slotted discs for big-time stopping power. The wheels are 18 inchers by Oasis Alloy Wheels.

Builder: Performance West Group

The 421-cubic inch Tri-Power engine was built by Van Gordon Racing and carries a multitude of aftermarket and upgraded parts, enabling it to produce a true 400 horsepower at 5,500 rpm. It has a compression ratio of 10:75 to 1.
Performance West

The stance of this Goat hauler is slightly forward thanks to the advanced suspension system.
Performance West

The custom interior sports Parchment Pearl leather seats sewn to the original '65 GTO pattern. The interior is fairly stock with a stock-appearing dash. All the metal pieces were supplied by YearOne.   Performance West

Performance Group West produced a dynamite 1965 Pontiac GTO Resto-Mod, coating it with Tiger Gold Pearl. The body has retained its original look—with the exception of 1966 Grand Prix driving lights.   Performance West

1968 PONTIAC FIREBIRD RESTO-MOD

It's really hard to determine why the Firebird is such a low-priority choice for Resto-Mod modification when compared to the Camaro.

Even though the body styling of the early Firebirds was totally identical to the Camaros, these models are rarely seen as Resto-Mods. This Firebird has all the ingredients of a Resto-Mod with a drag flavor.

A montage of chrome and polished aluminum on this engine just takes your breath away. It's a modern built-up 400 big block with aftermarket everything and is capable of over 500 horses.

Whatever the reason, it's certainly hard to argue the excellence of this 1968 Firebird Resto.

There is a significant power plant with a built-up Pontiac big block and a Competition Cam, Eagle Rods Headman Headers, aluminum heads and a .030-inch overbore. There is a competent transmission with a shift-kit equipped and upgraded 400 Turbo automatic and a custom 4.11 rear end.

The upgraded interior sports black high-back seats with blue inserts and the same color scheme also is carried into the trunk. The dash sports a nifty digital gauge package along with Vintage air conditioning, a Hurst Shifter and both custom door panels and console.

Note that there is a racing touch to this machine with a complete roll cage nicely fashioned inside. It's not that uncommon these days to see a Resto-Mod with that kind of competition look.

Builder: Mike Landis
Owner: Jeff Garlitz

The exterior has been retained in totally stock configuration with that classic grille still looking great after all these years. Note the subtle ghost flames that reach the length of the body sides.

The interior carries a modern flavor with the Grant tilt steering wheel, custom digital gauges, billet pedals plus the custom door panels and seats.

The rear view of this Judge Resto looks as good as the front. *Jefferson Bryant*

1969 PONTIAC GTO JUDGE RESTO-MOD

This striking '69 GTO Judge Resto-Mod has been on the pages of a national Pontiac magazine, and it's certainly deserving of the exposure.

Its Carousel Red body color with blue, red and yellow custom flamed hand-painted stripes are striking and bring excitement to the look of the vintage Judge.

But make no mistake, the look of performance on this hauler is more than skin deep. The power train is sturdy and powerful with a greater-than-400-horsepower, built-up Pontiac engine hooked to a Rick Armstrong custom-built M-22 Muncie four-speed tranny and 10-bolt Positraction rear end.

Underneath, there is suspension capable of handling the power with dropped spindles along with aftermarket Rancho bushings and other parts. The brakes are stainless-steel units with nifty orange powder-coated rotors. They stop a set of American Torque Thrust II Billet wheels, 17 inches in the front and three inches larger on the rear.

The interior is also first rate with a number of modern aftermarket additions. It's enough to make any Judge owner proud!

Builder: Red Line Auto Sports
Owner: Fred and Kim Martin

The Judge was the next step beyond the GTO in 1969 and this Judge Resto-Mod takes it one step higher! Its classic lines remain unchanged. Jefferson Bryant

The interior is an upgraded version of the original layout with the upholstery redone by the builder, carbon fiber Auto Meter gauges and a Sony sound system. Jefferson Bryant

1970 Pontiac GTO Resto-Mod

It's hard to put in words when describing the appearance of this GTO Resto-Mod. It's done to perfection in a PPG Aqua and the door handles and trunk lock have been shaved. The external look continues with one-off Coddington 18- and 20-inch spoke wheels.

The power plant is a killer based on a Pontiac 400 block with Pontiac 5C Heads, totally-aftermarket innards, a Pro-Charger P600B Supercharger with 11 pounds of boost and an MSD Crank Trigger.

The transmission is an upgraded Turbo400 automatic with a B&M 2800rpm stall converter. The rear end contains a Pontiac housing with Moser axles and Richmond 3.90 gears. Brakes are Baer units with 13.1/2-inch body color units.

The interior has Dakota Digital Gauges, a completely-clean custom dash, hand-built console containing a serious control system, Flow Fit custom seats, and custom fiberglass door panels covered with vinyl. And naturally, there's a pounding stereo system that features components from Sony, Precision Power and Boston Acoustics.

Owner: Chuck Hamly

The front end of this striking 1970 Pontiac GTO is a one-piece fiberglass part. The hood is also fiberglass and is attached with fasteners so it can be lifted off. Chuck Hamly

This engine has power but its appearance in the engine bay also is impressive. It is detailed to the hilt with lots of chrome and polished aluminum. The engine compartment has hand-made aluminum inner fenders. The firewall was shaved and the compartment was painted body color. Chuck Hamly

The custom interior matches the excellence of the exterior. All the switches and controls have been removed from the dash for a clean look. The touch screen for the console control system has an aluminum cover that slides over the screen when the ignition is turned off. The hand-made fiberglass door panels and rear side panels are wrapped in vinyl. Chuck Hamly

The first impression of this '70 Buick GSX is its stock appearance. But there are a number of Resto-Mod changes. Externally the wheels are 17-inch five-spoke Newstalgia models.   Todd Miller

1970 BUICK GSX RESTO-MOD

A vintage Buick muscle car isn't exactly what you would expect for a Resto-Mod conversion, but that's the case here.

The 1970 GSX is already one tough-looking machine, but it's been taken a number of steps further with this example.

The power train is modern high-tech with an LS2 engine hooked to an ATD 4L60E four-speed with a PTC 3800 stall converter, an aluminum driveshaft and a Moser Engineering 12-bolt rear end. The 17-inch Billet Buick rally wheels are by Newstalgia.

Wilwood lightweight discs do the stopping duties. The suspension is totally aftermarket with contributions coming from Edelbrock, QA-1, Global West and Speedtech Performance. On the dash, there are modern Auto Meter gauges and tach, and Vintage air conditioning.

Builder: AutoKraft
Owner: Todd Miller

Underneath this stock-appearing body are a number of modern suspension and power train upgrades.   Todd Miller

FORD RESTO-MODS

This BF Goodrich tire ad showed Resto-Mod customizer Chip Foose and his Mustang creation.

You have to look closely to tell if this is a 1960s customized Mustang or not. Actually it's a modern Resto-Mod version. The rich, deep paint is one telltale sign.

Quite frankly, possibly even more than Camaro in the Chevy camp, the Mustang rates extremely high in Resto-Mod conversions in the Ford camp. The percentage of Resto-Mod Fords could be as high as 75 percent Mustang.

No doubt, the influence of the Shelby continuation cars and the new Resto Mustang model played heavily into that choice. It's those early-year models that really get attention, the 1965 through 1968 models. Just about every conceivable external look and power trains have been assembled. That classic early 'Tang look will never be outdated. It really seems to flourish as a Resto-Mod with the larger wheels and low-profile tires seeming to create a more aggressive look.

It's hard to understand why the full-size muscle models of the period, such as the Fairlane, haven't enjoyed the popularity of the Chevy Chevelle in the Resto-Mod hobby.

1965 Mustang Coupe Resto-Mod

A unique homemade creation, this 1965 Mustang Coupe Resto-Mod sets some new directions with its design and home-brewed innovations. Owner/builder Justin Baker started with an interesting color combination of Prowler Orange and silver for the body covering, with popular Torque Thrust II wheels on the corners. It just knocks you out!

His built-up 302 Ford engine with all the goodies gets it done under the hood when it is combined with a reworked four-speed manual transmission hooked into a Hayes clutch. Out back, there is a more-modern eight-inch rear end.

Throughout the car, there are a number of beautifully crafted billet pieces that add a lot of class to this first-generation Mustang.

Suspension consists of aftermarket springs for ride height and stiffer leaf springs. An interesting innovation is in the trunk where a floor panel can be lifted revealing a storage area. Also, there are remote controls for both the hood release and gas cap.

Builder and owner: Justin Baker

The once neglected and aging Mustang now carries a dazzling Prowler Orange and silver paint job. It's one example of Resto-Mod attention, for sure.

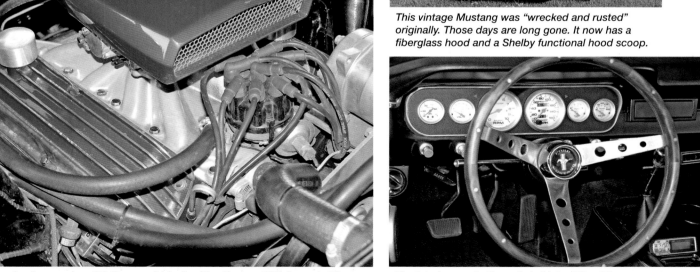

This vintage Mustang was "wrecked and rusted" originally. Those days are long gone. It now has a fiberglass hood and a Shelby functional hood scoop.

The engine is a modern 5.0-liter small block with a Demon 600cfm carb. The homemade internal scoop mirrors the outside scoop. It's capable of about 325 horses. Also included are aluminum valve and pulley covers. The valve covers and scoop carry the body color.

The interior sports these Auto Meter Ultra-Lite gauges plus a Hurst shifter, a stock-appearing Mustang wheel and a custom console by Mustangs Unlimited.

1965 Mustang Fastback Resto-Mod

If all the Mustang Resto-Mods looked as sharp as this K.A.R. Auto Group-built machine, probably a majority of all the Resto-Mods would be Mustangs. This model is as clean as a whistle!

The company calls this example its first STE Classic Mustang, exhibiting superior styling, technology and engineering. K.A.R. Auto Group succeeded on all counts.

Right off the bat, it's got a Shelby 'Tang look with the front end and wide white stripes. But even with that vintage look, just about everything else is modern.

First, there is the power train, headed by a modern 5.0-liter Ford crate engine that provides about 350 horses.

There's a five-speed and 3.55 gearing in the Currie rear end.

The interior is totally custom and done in a cold black. The gauges and steering wheel are all aftermarket and the bucket seats are the Rally reclining type. All the handles and knobs are billet aluminum. Out back, there is a 16-gallon Fuel Safe fuel cell.

The suspension is totally high tech with a Fat Man front adjustable-strut suspension and 200-pound rear leaf springs.

Builder and owner: K.A.R. Auto Group

This K.A.R. Auto Group-built 1965 Mustang typifies what the "Resto-Mod" term means today with the vintage body and modern engine, interior and suspension.

From the rear, this fastback Mustang looks like a 1960s road racer — especially with those dual white stripes.

A 5.0-liter Ford crate engine with 350 willing horses drives this classic Resto-Mod Mustang. It's hooked to a T5 five-speed transmission and a 3.55 Truetrac differential with 31 spline axles.

The interior is completely upgraded with a K.A.R. modular console, billet handles, pulls, pedals, custom-molded dash panel, custom white-face gauges, a Grant steering wheel, and a unique aluminum shifter.

1967 MUSTANG GT/R-CODE RESTO-MOD

When Performance West designed its 1967 Mustang GT/R Resto machine, the organization wanted to improve on this admired fastback design. The goals were to refine the handling and kick up the performance of the classic vehicle.

Horsepower was increased to 450 with a 4.6-liter 32-valve modern V-8 equipped with a twin-screw supercharger. Stopping this GT is accomplished by 13-inch SSBC Tri-Power disc brakes that bring the 18-inch lightweight wheels to a screeching halt.

The Performance West Group named this 1967 Mustang Fastback as its GT/R-Code Mustang. With its forward stance and multiple air intakes, it gives the impression of being all business. Performance West

The interior is toned in black and silver leather with red suede and is complete with a custom wheel. The cold black console features a custom shifter. *Performance West*

The engine is a modern 4.6-liter 32-valve Ford small block equipped with a Kenne Bell twin-screw supercharger that helps push out the 450 horsepower. It's done with an "all business" black and silver motif. *Performance West*

The bright exhaust tips from the cat-back dual-exhaust system are clearly in view from this angle, along with much of the rear suspension and undercarriage. *Performance West*

In addition, there is a modernized four-wheel independent suspension system that makes the GT/R-Code a superbly-balanced driving machine.

This modernized GT looks as great as it drives. The Billet Silver paint is accented by dark tinting that highlights the glass areas of the fastback. Inside, the excellence continues with an artful combination of leather and suede.

This Mustang Resto-Mod gets it done everywhere you look!

Builder: Performance West

1967 FASTBACK "NITEMARE" MUSTANG RESTO-MOD

The "Nitemare" name would probably be applicable for any vehicle that pulled alongside for a little stoplight challenge.

He or she would have to face over 600 horsepower with a solid power train carrying a Tremec TKO600 five-speed tranny, a Quarter-master steel driveshaft, and a Currie nine-inch rear end with a 3.50 gear ratio.

The looks of the model will shock anyone with its superb panel fitting, the shaved door handles and the black urethane base-coat clear-coat. Also, that black-oriented custom interior is beyond comparison.

Custom Classics built their 1967 "Nitemare" fastback Mustang with Billups Auto Body and produced this truly incredible Resto-Mod. The body is done in a cold black with the exhaust exiting just forward of the rear wheel cutouts. Silver racing stripes drop over the complete body. *Custom Classics*

Handling was also addressed in a big way with a Heidts Mustang II full suspension system and cross-member assembly. Air Ride Technologies provided the ride and airbag support system. Heidts also provided the front sway bar and adjustable proportioning valve. Wilwood donated the stopping mechanisms using four huge disc brakes equipped with six-piston aluminum calipers.

Builder: Custom Classics and Billups Auto Body

The interior features 2007 Mustang GT seats cut down to fit that are leather covered. It also has a custom center console, Auto Meter gauges, a Flaming River steering column and a custom high-power sound system. *Custom Classics*

This 1968 Reen Machine-built Resto-Mod Mustang exhibits the best of everything in resto characteristics. It's painted in Acapulco Blue, its original color. *Reenmachine*

1968 FORD MUSTANG FASTBACK RESTO-MOD

The body of this professionally built Mustang Fastback was blasted to bare metal and coated with premium show-quality Acapulco Blue paint. It carries all-new trim and chrome.

The power train contains a 5.0-liter GT-40 350 engine with 350 horsepower provided. The transmission is a Ford Racing World Class T-5 five-speed manual unit. It's hooked up to a custom aluminum driveshaft and a 2004 Mustang Cobra 8.8-inch 3.55:1-geared rear end.

The interior has a number of custom touches with updated three-point seat belts, a Reenmachine instrument cluster with Stewart-Warner black face gauges, a Flaming tilt column and a Grant mahogany steering wheel. The sweet sounds come from a complete Pioneer sound system.

Stopping is accomplished by aftermarket disc brakes on all four corners. The front suspension uses a Phase II McPherson strut system, Koni coil-overs, and a one-inch anti-roll bar. Out back, there's a 2004 Mustang Cobra independent rear suspension. The rubber to the road comes from 17-inch Michelin Pilot Sport ZPs, with the wheels from a late-model Ford Mach One Mustang.

Builder: Reenmachine

Power is 21st century with a new Ford Racing 5.0-liter GT-40 350-horsepower V-8. The induction system is a Mass-Flo air-type electronic fuel injection system. *Reenmachine*

The interior deploys a Reenmachine custom instrument cluster with Stewart-Warner black-face gauges, a Flaming River steering column, a Grant mahogany wheel and a Pioneer sound system, among other upgrades.   *Reenmachine*

CHAPTER 6

CHRYSLER RESTO-MODS

Watch any national collectible car auction, and you will note something about the popularity of Mopar muscle cars.

First of all, it goes without saying that any of those 1960s and '70s models carrying a 426-Hemi engine will be drawing a multitude of bidders and huge money.

Also, there are a number of body styles, when combined with the Hemi, that can produce selling prices in the seven-figure range! Probably the top model and engine combination is the 1970 and 1971 Hemi 'Cuda, but Chargers and Challengers with big engines also draw big dollars.

The same can be said for the top-money Resto-Mods with the Chrysler label. In a recent auction, a pristine Hemi 'Cuda brought a big-time $240,000! And right behind it was a Resto-Mod Hemi 'Cuda using a body that could well have been sitting on a six-cylinder-engine chassis. No matching numbers here, and the Hemi that sat under the hood was a new crate engine. But the crowd loved it, and it brought $80,000!

Certainly, in today's world, there are a small percentage of Mopar fans who can afford a Hemi car. Their price is just out of sight, but so is the experience of owning a stock-appearing Mopar Resto-Mod.

The connection of the 'Cuda and others to high performance has manifested itself in some Mopar Resto-Mod conversions. A popular creation has been to mate a 'Cuda body with a V-10 Viper V-10 500-horsepower engine.

How's that for making the best of the Resto-Mod concept?

1967 PLYMOUTH BARRACUDA

When he was a teenager, Tom Merkt inherited a 1967 Barracuda from his sister, but over the course of time it got away from him. Later, through a friend, he located another one for sale and he sure didn't let this one get away.

Being the owner of his own body shop, he was the guy to accomplish this amazing Resto-Mod conversion. First, every seam was stitch-welded for total smoothness. A new front end was installed with new inner fenders. A roll cage was installed making the vintage Mopar as solid as a rock.

This Mothers® car wax ad showed a 1971 'Cuda Resto-Mod called the G-Force 'Cuda.

Here is a model that you don't often see receiving Resto-Mod treatment. This 1967 Plymouth Barracuda really gets it done! All seams were stitch-welded to make the body more rigid. Tom Merkt

The highlight of this Mopar machine is under the hood where there is a 630-cube 440 Magnum crate engine. It's clean and has most of the wiring and plumbing hidden. Note the triple master cylinder set-up. *Tom Merkt*

The suspension is also up to the task with Magnum Force tubular A-arms and coil-overs up front and a set of modern leaf springs out back. Stout sway bars keep everything in place front and rear.

The power train is impressive, to say the least, with a built-up 440 mill that pushes out in excess of 600 ponies. On down the line are an 833 Hemi four-speed and a SureGrip-equipped 8-3/4-inch rear end that can easily blur 17-inch Volk wheels.

The interior is totally custom and on the quality level of the rest of the machine. In the land of Resto-Mods, this effort stands very tall!

Builder and owner: Tom Merkt

Everything is done in black and white vinyl. For safety, there is a five-point seat belt system. The stock dash is augmented with Auto Meter gauges. *Tom Merkt*

This YearOne promotional photo shows a Resto-Mod creation highlighting the black rear signboard carrying the 505 Wedge identification. *YearOne*

1969 PLYMOUTH ROAD RUNNER RESTO-MOD

This particular Resto-Mod was constructed by YearOne for more of a "go" than a "show" motivation. The machine was tested at Putnam Park Road Course in Indiana during Air Ride Technologies' annual Street Challenge event. Using that suspension system, the "Red Runner," as it was called, really showed its stuff! The Plymouth was garbed in a Resto-Mod motif with a 505-cubic-inch engine, upgraded performance and suspension, along with a custom interior. You gotta love it!

Builder and owner: YearOne

This pumped-up 505-cubic-inch Mopar crate engine is capable of a solid 510 horses. It is balanced and blueprinted, carries forged pistons and crank, roller rockers, Edelbrock aluminum heads and a modified Six-Pack air cleaner. *YearOne*

The interior was updated with modern gauges, steering wheel and a custom shifter. *YearOne*

YearOne called this Resto-Mod the "Red Runner," a color that was carried throughout the model. *YearOne*

1970 DODGE CHALLENGER RESTO-MOD

It seems that one of the attributes of today's Resto-Mods is a bright color scheme. This 1970 Dodge Challenger, though, bucks that trend with this subtle white and gray motif. The custom interior features a white-face gauge package and a composite dash. There's modern Hemi power under the hood with a 6.1-liter version of the famous engine. Underneath, it's just as good as it is on the topside, detailed out to perfection.

Builder and owner: Dave Weber

This 1970 Dodge Challenger Resto-Mod varies from the bright colors that made the brand so popular in its heyday. The body is highlighted with a subtle silver striping. *Roadster Shop*

High technology is on the dash plate with a composite dash and modern white-face gauges. In addition, check out that custom three-spoke wheel. *Roadster Shop*

The silver rear stripe is interesting and it looks like a continuation of the rear chrome bumper. The silver detailing also blends neatly with the chrome wheels. *Roadster Shop*

The vaunted Hemi name is present on this Resto-Mod in the form of a modern Mopar crate engine with 6.1 liters involved in this example. *Roadster Shop*

1970 Dodge Challenger Resto-Mod

This totally wild Dodge Challenger requires quite awhile to totally absorb the overpowering fabrication and technology of the beast. Every aspect of the machine pushes the technology.

First, there's that engine that pumps out over 1,300 horsepower when the nitrous system is included. Everything else in the power train remains modern with a five-speed Kiesler transmission and a Fab 9 Detroit Locker rear end.

The suspension is by Magna Force with an air ride system. Stopping is accomplished by 12-inch Wilwood disc brakes. Open the doors and you will view one of the finest interiors ever, done by Paul Atkins. It might not look like it, but the owner assures that this is a street-legal Resto-Mod.

Builders: Advanced Chassis, Koffel's Place and Robert and Chris Motz

Owner: Robert Motz

The interior is totally custom with leather seats, Auto Meter Cobalt gauges, a Colorado Customs steering wheel plus a leather console.

This 1970 Challenger Resto-Mod sports a completely-stock body, but beyond that, this is one wild and crazy Mopar machine.

The colors Sexy Candy Apple Red and Black Cherry set off this powerful hauler in a big way. Note the forward rake of the body stance.

The gold-leaf lettering advertises the Hemi engine size.

That's a carbureted 550-cubic-inch Keith Black Hemi engine that is capable of 810 horsepower. But that's not all. In the trunk is a 500-horse NOS nitrous system providing an additional 500 horsepower. The engine detailing is immaculate in chrome and body color.

1968 Dodge Dart Resto-Mod

Bet you've never seen a vintage Dodge Dart that has the style and personality of this Schwartz Extreme Performance-built machine. It's high-tech and innovation throughout.

First, there's that nifty paint scheme that features PPG "Street Silk" and a modern PPG Vibrance orange shade. There's also a unique multi-color stripe that divides the colors.

Suspension was a strong consideration in the building of this Mopar machine, with a Heidts independent rear suspension modified by Schwartz. Alterkation front suspension, also modified by the builder, features coil-over shocks and custom sub-frame connectors.

Then there is the stuff that makes this Chrysler hauler get down the road. The 528 Hemi crate engine has received significant modifications, including internal reworking and a custom EFI with dual four-barrel throttle bodies. Add to that a port-injected NOS system and you've got almost 800 horses at your right foot.

The transmission is a Bowler-built 4L80E four-speed connected to a Twist Machine paddle shifter. The rear end is a Heidts 3.90 Positraction. The power train drives 18-inch forged aluminum wheels.

Builder: Schwartz Extreme Performance

This Dart Resto-Mod carries the "Poison Dart" name and it's very appropriate. The body is done in an orange and white design with yellow and black modern graphics. Jeff Schwartz

The engine compartment is a combination of beauty and brute performance. The 528 Hemi crate engine features dual throttle-body injection plus a Port-Injected Nitrous System. Jeff Schwartz

This 1968 Dart Resto-Mod has the best of everything with the magnificent work being performed by Schwartz Performance. The body remained stock but the innovative color scheme gives it an entirely different look. Jeff Schwartz

RESTO-MOD PICKUP TRUCKS AND STATION WAGONS

"Great 'rides' are not born, they're created."

Foose 100

Chip Foose
*Award winning automotive
designer and builder*

For that perfect non-compromising shine,
pick up Mothers® products
at your local automotive retailer today.

MOTHERS®
Polishes•Waxes•Cleaners

mothers.com
detailguide.com • waxforum.com

This Mothers® car wax ad shows the Foose 100 pickup. That proves the Resto-Mod trend isn't just for cars!

So you think that all the vehicles involved in the Resto-Mod craze are cars? That's true to a large extent, but the trend is happening to pickups at an increasing rate during the early years of the 21st century.

But there are differences between the two types of vehicles.

First of all, the vehicle ages of cars usually falls in the 1950s, 1960s and 1970s decades. With the pickup trucks intended for transformation, the truck's age starts a couple decades earlier—in the 1930s—and reaches into the 1950s. Once in awhile there is a rare 1960s version.

The comparison is interesting in that the car Resto-Mods are using more modern styling while the old high-cab classic pickups give an entirely different impression. While purists object to any kind of modification to classic vehicles, they certainly can't object too much as those vintage bodies stay pretty much the same with the Resto conversion.

All of the Big Three carmakers have their followings with the Resto-Mod automobile versions, but that isn't the same with their pickup counterparts.

The same basic rules apply to the light trucks as they do to the cars and that means a stock body, a modern power train and a revised interior.

Also a part of this category for purposes of this book are truck-like vehicles including station wagons and sedan delivery-type vehicles.

1934 FORD PICKUP RESTO-MOD

It's more than seven decades old but it has only looked like this Resto-Mod version for a small percentage of that time. John Whip has owned it for two of those decades and is responsible for the changes.

Like most vintage pickup Restos, there isn't a totally new engine here, but it is over 40 years newer than the original flathead. The remainder of the power train is also more modern with a 350 turbo automatic transmission and a Ford Granada eight-inch rear end.

The interior is top drawer with modern parts and pieces everywhere you look. Chrome, cherry wood and tweed materials are all there in abundance!

And here is the nice part of this story: The owner did a majority of the work himself!

Builder and owner: John Whip

The modernized interior is done in a dark and light maroon tweed. All door handles, pedals and steering column are all modern. The stock body-color dash contains Classic Gauges with a LaCarra steering wheel.

Power comes from a 350 Chevy V-8 that is 35 years newer than the truck. It provides serious power to this vintage 2,500-pound vehicle.

The classic factory lines of this 1934 Ford pickup have been retained. Combined with the custom wheels and red grille, this is one sharp one-off Resto-Mod.

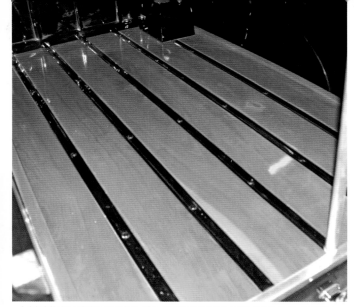

A highlight of the truck is the natural wood with dark metal strips. That's not the normal battery location in the upper right corner.

The rear view of this 1934 Ford pickup shows the high-mounted brake light built into the custom bed cover, its lack of a rear bumper and the period blue-dot taillights.

No cutting was done on this original 1941 Chevy truck. This pickup's lines are intact.

This impressive grille, a combination of vertical and horizontal chrome strips, might look like it came from a custom shop but it's the original 1941 Chevy front-end design.

1941 CHEVY PICKUP RESTO-MOD

It has an old-school look (well, at least partially) with subtle flames on the front fenders and hood. Otherwise, the Catalina Blue body is pretty much stock and is totally uncut. Sitting in that pristine bed much of the time is a restored vintage midget race car that really gives the truck a great look.

The small block Chevy engine is about three decades newer than the truck with its performance monitored by modern VDO gauges. They are just a part of the custom interior done in tan leather. Modern 13/12-inch brakes get it stopped quickly. Owner Roger Robinson also added a number of his own billet pieces and did much of the work on the truck build-up himself.

Builder and owner: Roger Robinson

The rear end features some of the owner's handiwork with the taillight bracket, gas cap and horns being fabricated in aluminum.

The interior has been modernized with white-face VDO gauges on the stock dash and a more-modern steering wheel. And check out that sporty Chevy Bowtie brake pedal!

1947 GMC PICKUP RESTO-MOD

A vintage GMC pickup is very similar to a Chevy, but you just don't see many of them accepting a Resto-Mod conversion.

Owner Wayne Carrier admitted that this beauty was a "barn find" in the early 2000s. "It was not a pretty sight with big-time rust and bird droppings. It had been in there for at least 10 years, but everything was there, so I gave the owner the $600 he asked for to drag it out."

The before and after of this vintage GMC are shown by the artwork. The ratty blue starting point is illustrated complete with the bird doo-doo on the left with today's masterpiece on the right.

The front end of this 1947 GMC pickup is totally stock including the grille. Note the parking lights directly below the headlights where "GMC" is cut out and replaced by an opaque plastic that is illuminated when the running lights are turned on.

The interior features 2000 Caddy charcoal leather seats and a stock body-color dash with Dolphin Gauges. Open the stock glove box door and you will see a DVD player and screen. The steering system features a Flaming River wheel and a modern tilt system.

This is a 1985 IROC Chevy V-8 engine that has been considerably upgraded with a Holly Fuel Injection System and a bored-out plenum for better air flow.

Besides the upgraded 1985 IROC Camaro engine, there's a modern 700R4 automatic transmission with overdrive and an IROC 10-bolt rear end.

It's that very-close-to-stock body that really blows you away with its unique Chrysler Deep Cranberry and almost invisible ghost stripes.

As Resto-Mods go, this is a low-budget machine. Just goes to show what you can do without a pile of money.

Builder and owner: Wayne Carrier

1948 Chevy Pickup Resto-Mod

If Chevy had built its 1948 pickup to look like this one, they would probably still be produced. This Mercedes Silver machine is the best of every aspect of the Resto-Mod hobby.

The body is so perfect, it looks like it was molded of silver. The original body lines have been preserved, but it just takes on a different look. Quite frankly, it is perfect!

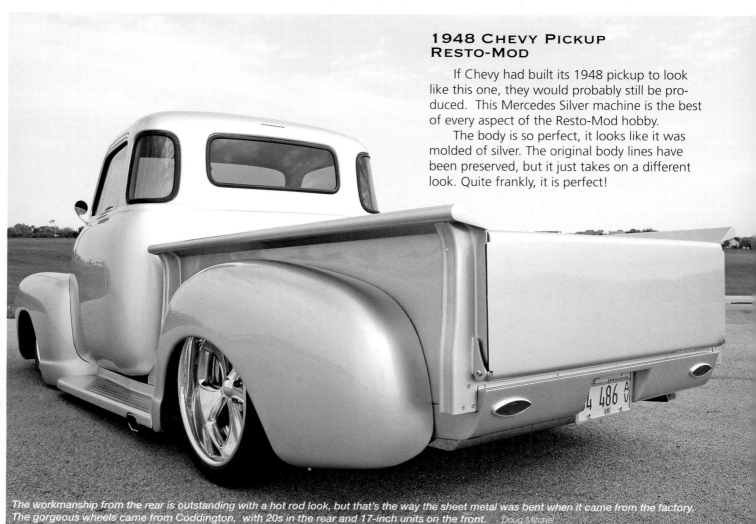

The workmanship from the rear is outstanding with a hot rod look, but that's the way the sheet metal was bent when it came from the factory. The gorgeous wheels came from Coddington, with 20s in the rear and 17-inch units on the front. *Doug Mitchel*

Then there is that killer engine compartment. There is power and unbelievable detailing. The body color of the compartment and the chrome and aluminum detailing on the 502 GM crate engine light up the night.

The power plant might be beautiful, but it's potent and connected to a modern 700R4 trans and a Currie Positraction rear end.

The chassis holds it all together with a custom front clip and a triangulated four-link system out back. There's also an air ride to smooth the travel with giant Wilwood discs bringing it to a quick stop.

Owner: Jeff and Brenda Kuhn

Power comes from a 502 GM Performance Crate Engine. It seems everything possible is either polished aluminum or chrome. The molding surrounding the radiator was fabricated. Doug Mitchel

An interesting location for the Classic Instruments gauges was putting them in the center of the custom dash. Doug Mitchel

The big block engine is a 1993 454 Chevy V-8 with twin Edelbrock 500 carbs and aluminum intake and a 10:1 compression ratio. The owner estimated that it produces 500 horsepower.

The stock-appearing hood and fenders are fiberglass and feature a unique bumper pivoting arrangement allowing easy access to the engine compartment.

1954 Ford F-100 Resto-Mod Pickup

Owner Gene Powers bought this "beauteous" Ford pickup in 1989 and used it for five years as a working truck. In 1994, he started his restoration, an effort that required a dozen years.

He retained the stock look of the working machine with all those classic lines surviving intact. The lines might be intact, but we have to admit that the hood and fenders are all one piece and swing forward off the front of the truck completely exposing the engine compartment. It's done in a gorgeous Teal color.

And quite an engine it is, with some 500 ponies at the waiting! A 400 turbo automatic with a shift kit and a newer nine-inch Ford Positraction rear end complete the power train.

The front suspension is based on a 1976 Nova front clip with aftermarket coil springs and modern gas shocks. In the rear, there are modern leaf springs and gas shocks. In an interesting touch, the rear axle was mounted on top of the leaf springs.

The interior is modernized in great fashion with a number of upgrades.

You gotta love everything about it!

Builder and owner: Gene Powers

The stock look of this 1954 Ford F-100 was mostly retained, but there are slight changes with a 1956 grille and side Ford emblems.

The factory look continues from this angle with a custom rear bumper and the exhaust tips emerging from under the rear of the running boards.

1956 FORD (BIG BACK WINDOW) RESTO-MOD PICKUP

It's uncut, an important "in" for vintage pickup Resto-Mod fans. That outward appearance grabs you immediately with the dramatic Dupont Torch Red covering. Add those classic Coddington wheels (17-inch front and an inch bigger out back) and you have a crowd stopper of the first order.

The power train gets it done with an upgraded Ford small block with Demon carburetion, a reworked Ford C-6 tranny and a nine-inch Ford rear end.

Suspension is high tech with a Mustang II front end and four-link in the rear. They are both coupled with an air ride set-up and there are discs on all four corners. The custom interior is by Dan Wickett while the bed is walnut with stainless-steel strips. It's truly a fantasy Resto truck!

Builder: Hot Rod Construction
Owner: Ricky Black

The engine is a modernized 351 Ford V-8 that is presented in a greatly chromed condition. It carries a fire-vehicle theme with a vintage fire helmet and siren mounted on the engine.
Hot Rod Construction

This 1956 Ford F-100 Resto-Mod pickup shows the classic factory body of this model year. The only change is carrying the body color to the running boards. Hot Rod Construction

The custom flamed steering wheel is an eye-catching creation.
Note the VDO white-faced gauges.   Hot Rod Construction

This truck doesn't have a traditional truck bed. It's here in the form of a clear plastic floor. It allows viewing the undercarriage craftsmanship. *Hostottle*

Owner Steve Haessly knows what he's doing when he performs the Resto-Modding process on old Ford trucks. All the trim and door handles have been removed with classy smoothing and molding. *Hostottle*

1956 Ford F-100 Resto-Mod

In terms of fabrication, modification and excellence, it doesn't get much better than this Ford Resto-Mod. It has a different treatment than the previous example.

The body smoothing is beyond reproach but it does not compromise the vintage body lines. The power plant is certainly up to the test of pushing this pickup, with 550 horsepower, an upgraded Ford C-6 tranny, and a Winters nine-inch Ford rear end. Excellence is everywhere with Boyd Coddington wheels, a clear bed floor, aftermarket frame and suspension system, and an out-of-sight custom interior. It's like a glass of fine 50-year-old wine, just too valuable to drink, and in the case of this truck, too valuable to drive?

Owner: Steve Haessly

An aluminum-headed 460 Ford big block provides huge horses. The engine is a masterpiece with every external component either chromed or polished. It all fits neatly under the stock hood. Hostottle

Everything has been upgraded to perfection in the cockpit: custom dash with modern gauges, chrome steering column by Budnik and modern white leather seats. Hostottle

1956 CHEVY 3100 RESTO-MOD PICKUP

With a design that looked ahead of its time, the '56 Chevy pickup looked great then and makes a great-looking Resto-Mod now. The Prell aluminum wheels just seem to blend with the sleek model.

Power is provided by a more modern, built-up 283-cid Chevy V-8. A perfect power train match is a two-speed Powerglide transmission and a late-model Nova rear end. There are also 1990 Caddy tailpipes and 1950 Buick taillights.

The upgraded interior stands tall and is done in a gorgeous red velvet. It's also a cool driver with a 1976 Volaré front end (with parallel torsion bars) and air shocks in the back.

It's been a popular machine in car show competition and has taken many first places. The beauty of the truck is it has been a low-budget machine, something that a person can build without breaking the bank.

Builder: Bill Masters and Bill Masters Jr.
Owner: Evan Gillette

This 1956 Chevy pickup presents a solid factory look with a few exceptions. There have been a number of interesting Resto-Mod additions. The 15-inch slotted wheels are by Prell.

Upgrades include the sliding rear window, the wooden pickup bed with shiny strips and the diamond-plate tool box.

A later-version 283 V-8 engine was modernized with an Edelbrock cam and a Holley four-barrel 600cfm carb. Period Cherry Bomb mufflers give it a sweet sound!

1967 Chevy C-10 Resto-Mod Pickup

This Fesler Bolt pickup is one of the newest we've seen to receive the Resto-Mod treatment. It's a top effort with a heavy use of aluminum detailing. The power train is top drawer with a GM LQ4 6.0-liter Cadillac Escalade engine hooked to a blown GM 4L65E custom-built tranny and a built 12-bolt rear end.

The chassis features a Mustang II front end built into the full-boxed tube frame. The ride is smoothed with an Air Ride Technologies system.

It's truck perfection to the hilt, and certainly something that you would never want to perform any carrying tasks.

Builder: Fesler Built

Power for this Chevy pickup Resto-Mod comes from a blown GM LQ4 6.0-liter Escalade engine built by Arizona Speed and Marine. *Fesler Built*

The interior sports Auto Meter gauges in a custom-fab dash, a Teas Designs custom seat, a Colorado Customs steering wheel and Vintage Air A/C. *Fesler Built*

This 1967 Chevy C-10 Resto-Mod pickup sports a nearly-stock body with the exception of the hood-mounted protrusion and deletion of body trim. *Fesler Built*

1968 Chevy C-10 Resto-Mod Pickup

It's another superb Resto-Mod pickup truck and it was constructed by its owner, Rick Parsons, in just two years.

Power was certainly a consideration in this project with its 400-horsepower small-block Chevy V-8 matched to a Saginaw close-ratio four-speed manual tranny with a 3.53 Positraction rear end.

Stopping quickly and safely was also a consideration to the builder, with modern stock GM 11-inch front discs with the same size Cadillac units on the back.

The suspension is a high-tech Air Technologies system that allows up-and-down adjustment from close to the ground to about eight inches high. The two-inch difference in the American Racing Torque Thrust wheels gives the vehicle an aggressive stance.

The unique exterior color is matched nicely with the custom interior with a Covan dash, IDIDIT steering column and a billet Lecarra steering wheel.

Builder and owner: Rick Parsons

The interior sports a custom dash with modern Auto Meter Pro-Com gauges, 1980 Pontiac Fiero seats and other upgrades.

The engine is a greatly upgraded, modern 350 Chevy single four-barrel version. It's capable of about 400 horsepower with a Comp Cam. It's been detailed with aluminum valve covers and air cleaner cover.

While the Chevy CST pickup sports a very original body, the Resto-Mod influence offers this lower-than-original stance. It's one sharp Chevy Resto-Mod.

1955 CHEVY SEDAN DELIVERY RESTO-MOD

Randy Mack acquired this Sedan Delivery in 1987, "...completely shot except for the interior." The current restoration was completed in 2007.

It shows expertise from every angle with a modern LS-6 'Vette power plant equipped with a Lingenfelter intake. The tranny is a GM 4L60E automatic with a 1996 Corvette C4 rear end. The custom chassis was fabricated by Progress Automotive.

Brakes are 11-inch SSBC Discs. The Torch Red body has been cleaned of all chrome, and it generates interest from all ages. The interior is done in beige Ultra Leather, covering the rear seats from a 1957 Chevy Nomad wagon and the front is from a 1990 Dodge Daytona. Classic white-face gauges adorn the striped billet dash.

Builder and owner: Randy Mack

The stock dash has been highly modified with modern gauges and a billet stripe. The custom console mates with the dash and contains the sound system and shifter.

You gotta love the look of this 1955 Chevy Sedan Delivery Resto-Mod. The stock body is still intact but it's been stripped of practically all of the external chrome and trim pieces.
Randy Mack

In its time, the 1955 Chevy Sedan Delivery was designed for small-business uses. Today, in this Resto-Mod life, the vehicle is far beyond any of those purposes.
Randy Mack

These 17-inch Coddington aluminum wheels are the finishing touch to the out-of-sight external appearance of the '55 Chevy Sedan Delivery.

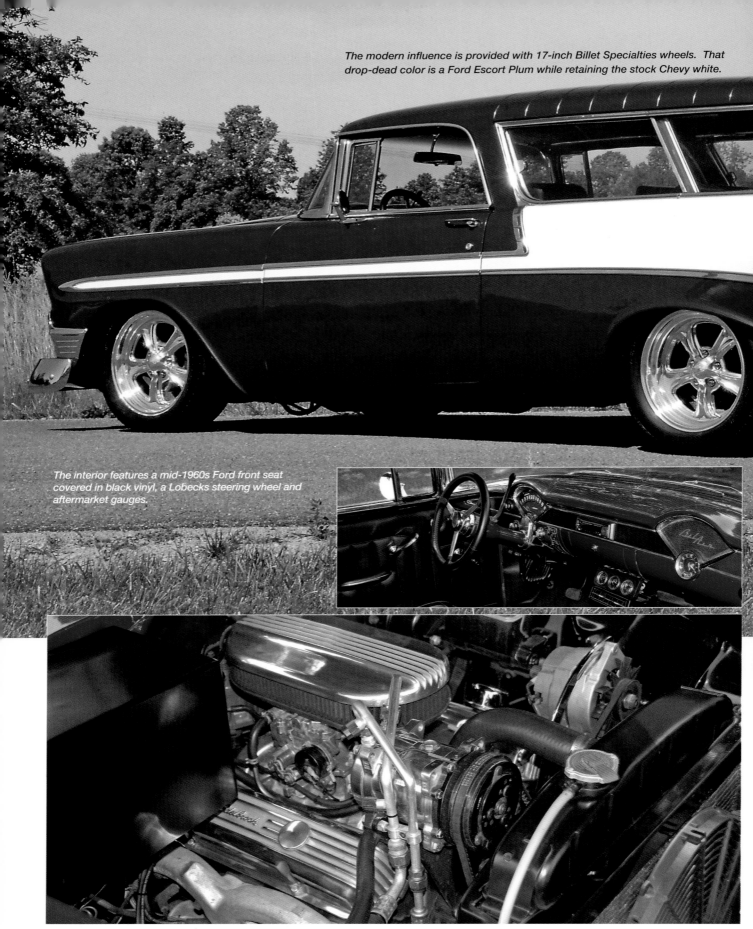

The modern influence is provided with 17-inch Billet Specialties wheels. That drop-dead color is a Ford Escort Plum while retaining the stock Chevy white.

The interior features a mid-1960s Ford front seat covered in black vinyl, a Lobecks steering wheel and aftermarket gauges.

Sitting in the engine compartment is a GM Performance 350 crate engine that has been detailed in chrome and aluminum. Its horsepower matches its displacement number.

1956 Chevy Nomad Resto-Mod

Owner Charlene Baker explained that she got her flashy 1956 Chevy Nomad in the early 2000s just about the way it appears in this book. It retains its external factory look, but why would you want to change that classic appearance?

There is power aplenty with a 350 GM crate engine that is hooked to an upgraded 350 turbo transmission with some shifting improvements. The rear end is a modern Hayes unit with 3.08 gears, but with a stock housing.

The plum and white beauty sports modern disc brakes on the front, but plans call for placing them on the rear. The wheels are striking 17-inch aluminum Chicaynes.

The advanced suspension system incorporates two-inch drop spindles along with aftermarket coil springs and modern shocks on the front. The rear highlights Posey leaf springs and modern shocks.

There are a number of subtle interior upgrades with black vinyl upholstery, a Lobecks steering wheel, aftermarket gauges and new dash trim.

Builder: Baker's Vintage Automotive
Owner: Charlene Baker

Even though it's a station wagon body, the classic 1957 tail fins still generate considerable interest. The 17-inch Boyd Coddington wheels are a nifty addition to this machine.

Many Resto-Mods substitute paint for chrome script. This gold leaf and green "Chevrolet" rendering blends beautifully with the car's appearance.

1957 Chevy Two-Ten Four-Door Wagon Resto-Mod

You wouldn't expect a four-door Chevy Two-Ten wagon to be the recipient of all the lavish treatment needed for a Resto-Mod conversion. But what Willy Murray accomplished with this working-style vehicle is amazing. That Winter Mint and White Diamond Pearl paint scheme is striking.

The power train isn't in the hundreds-of-horses category but it is potent with a more

This unlikely Resto-Mod, a 1957 Chevy 210 four-door station wagon, is covered by a classy combination of Winter Mint and White Diamond Pearl.

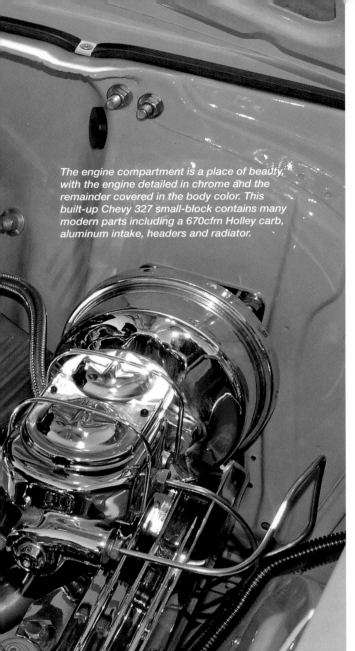

The engine compartment is a place of beauty, with the engine detailed in chrome and the remainder covered in the body color. This built-up Chevy 327 small-block contains many modern parts including a 670cfm Holley carb, aluminum intake, headers and radiator.

modern Chevy 327 providing 350 ponies. The transmission is a modern 700R four-speed with overdrive and the rear end sports 3.55 gearing.

There are front disc brakes to get this heavy hauler stopped. All the chrome detailing was retained, and check out that hand-painted "1957" on the rear quarter. Finally, there are those classy 17-inch Coddington Wheels on all four corners.

The interior might be the highlight of the machine. There's tan vinyl throughout with a 1999 Bonneville front seat. The steering column is by IDIDIT and Lecarra is the name on the steering wheel.

Add Auto Meter white-face gauges, a stainless steel dash strip, billet handles and a Mega sound system and everything is very, very cool!

Builder and owner: Willy Murray

The interior is modern to the hilt with an IDIDIT steering column, Lecarra steering wheel, Auto Meter white-face gauges, stainless steel dash strip and leather seats.

1959 CHEVROLET SEDAN DELIVERY RESTO-MOD

This is an unlikely selection for a Resto-Mod conversion, but it's an example that carries the cool name of "Winged Express." Even though it's a utilitarian hauler, you have to admit that what's been done really gets to you.

The Performance West Group calls this 1959 Chevy Sedan Delivery Resto-Mod the "Winged Express." The color is a delicious light tan accentuated by a deep tint on the windows. The low stance and the filled-in rear side windows give the working vehicle a long and lean look.
Performance West

This Turn Key-built LS2 Chevy Crate Engine is built up to the hilt with a twin-screw Kenne Bell supercharger mounted on top and providing a ground-pounding 750 horsepower. The detailing of the engine compartment is inspiring, with total chrome and polished aluminum covering almost everything. *Performance West*

First, there's that vivid Candy Red, exactly the correct amount of chrome, and of course, those characteristic 1959 Chevy rear wings.

The power train has unexpected performance with a modern 750-horsepower Chevy LS2 engine that is supercharged and intercooled. It has a tranny to accept those big horses with a modern six-speed Tremec overdrive unit. There is also a Hurst shifter and Centerforce clutch.

The interior is a masterpiece with an audio and video system by Sony, a modified dash, leather seats, and a cool breeze comes from a Vintage Air Performance A/C system.

The suspension is high-tech with an Air Ride system, augmented with Hotchkiss Sway Bars and SSBC Force-10 15-inch disc brakes.

Builder: Performance West Group

Open the doors and there is a set of 1963 Impala SS buckets and a matching center console. The seats are leather coated. The stylish dash has been upgraded with Impala bright trim. There are also additional modern gauges and Vintage air conditioning. *Performance West*

1968 PLYMOUTH GTX STATION WAGON RESTO-MOD

This Plymouth station wagon Resto-Mod was actually up-graded from stock in the late 1960s. It then was passed around before it came on hard times and was located sitting forlornly in a back yard where it had been neglected for a decade.

The wagon was meticulously brought back to and beyond its former glory by the Performance West Group. The power train consists of a reworked legendary 440 Six-Pack V-8, a heavy-duty Hayes Clutch and a A833 Hurst-shifted four-speed tranny.

Handling was a big priority for this Resto-Mod, with modern Eaton Detroit leaf springs front and rear, heavy duty torsion bars and Edelbrock IAS Performer Shocks. Also, SSBC Force-10 Tri-Power disc brakes are in place on all four corners.

Builder: Performance West Group

The external rear view shows the wagon to look pretty much stock, but it is carrying the distinctive GTX lower body stripe that reaches to the middle of the rear doors. Performance West

Even though this 1968 GTX conversion started as a station wagon, the changes made during this "restofication" have completely changed it into a tough-appearing Resto-Mod muscle machine. Performance West

The car has been updated with an authentic GTX interior, with the seats covered with hand-sewn white leather. The stock console holds a modern Hurst competition shifter. The modern external paint covers all the interior surfaces. There is also a Rallye Instrument panel. Performance West

The station wagon was enhanced with the scoop-bearing, lift-off hood. The Plymouth hauler is painted a B-5 Super Blue, very close to the original color. It's really set off by the Hurst-style Oasis wheels and the bright red caliper of the Tri-Power disc brakes. Performance West

CHAPTER 8

OLD CAR RESTO-MODS

The Resto-Mod trend has also made its way into more vintage machines, predominantly 1930s, '40s and '50s models. It's a trend that could continue to increase in interest. Not surprisingly, Fords and Chevys are the most popular for this application.

Basically the same ground rules apply here, with a few deviations. It seems that much of the upgrading here doesn't always go to current modern parts and pieces. More often, you will find the original engine being replaced by one that is 30 to 40 years newer. The same might also occur with other major pieces.

The body is retained in stock trim, with the wheels and tires somewhat smaller than the large extremes noted for the modern Resto-Mods.

The normal use of these Resto-Mods in earlier years was as street rods with their tops chopped several inches and the body channeled an equal amount. The appearance obviously was greatly changed, but that is not the case here.

An interesting popular engine player in this type of resto vehicle is the Cadillac V-8. Several examples in this chapter have used that powerful engine, including one with a 1997 32-valve Cadillac North Star engine being mated with a 1941 Caddy. Also, a pair of 1949 and 1950 Mercury Resto-Mods are using 1970s-vintage Caddy mills to power them down the road.

This 1929 Ford Coupe sports its completely stock look and is smoothed to perfection. All the chrome has been removed, and the headlight housings contain modern Halogen units. The top was fashioned by the owner out of a dark beige material supported by aluminum stringers.

1929 Ford Coupe Resto-Mod

The external look of this Frost Beige Resto-Mod is totally stock. By the way, those are the original headlight shells, but they are carrying modern halogen bulbs. The body is super smoothed with hidden hinges for the doors. Also, the rear window goes up and down. Is this neat?

The original frame is still in place, but it's been boxed for both appearance and strength. Undercarriage parts and pieces include four-inch drop axles by Super Bell, Pete and Jake Shocks and Alden coil-overs on the rear.

The engine is an interesting combination of the old and new. First, there's a modern Chevy crate engine joined by an original Offenhouser Tri-Power set-up with Rochester carbs. The transmission is a Saginaw four-speed and the vehicle uses a sprint car racing Halibrand differential.

Fuel comes from auxiliary fuel tanks that are located under the splash pans. The actual fuel cap is located in the rumble seat area.

Builder: Baker's Vintage Automotive
Owner: Brian Baker

The body color is carried into the engine compartment that contains a GM 350-cid, 350-horse crate engine. It's been equipped with an original-style Offy intake manifold with three two-barrel Rochester carbs. The homemade air cleaner cover is detailed in aluminum and body color.

The old rumble seat is still in position, but it never looked like this! That's the gas filler cap on the left side. The seats are total custom units.

The cleanness of the design continues in the rear with lower slotted taillights, revised license plate location and a workable top rear window.

1931 Chrysler Imperial Limousine Resto-Mod

Its huge size just overwhelms any viewer. The overall length probably reaches about 16 feet! This restoration of a grand 1930s machine took four long years and it looks it with all the excellence in these lines. That magnificent body coating is Lexus Black base coat and clear-coat-topped layers.

Much of the originality of the vintage Chrysler was retained, with the only deviation being a slight chop of the top. The original frame was also used, but it was boxed back to the firewall for extra strength.

The suspension is based on modern technology with Fat Man coil-over shocks on each corner. The original cross members are still in place.

The Viper V-10 engine under the hood is part of a potent power train that also includes a six-speed Viper transmission, a racing-style driveshaft, and a Pro Stock dragster-style locker rear end.

The interior is done in a gray cloth with six Stewart-Warner aftermarket gauges, and the original shifter rod still doing its thing. The steering column came from a Chevy S-10 and the steering wheel came from Colorado Classics. It even matches the styling of the wheels.

One of the most-asked questions about the monster restoration of this beautiful Chrysler Imperial comes when it is displayed—"What is it??"

Builder: Tom Ratliff
Owner: Mary Ratliff

This view shows the familiar luggage box located above the rear bumper. The turn signals are located on the back of the box.

The Viper V-10 Mopar engine is appropriate for this vintage Chrysler Resto-Mod. It takes plenty of power to push this monster along, but its 500 horses do the job nicely.

It's long and lean and carries a near stock appearance. It brings back the Prohibition time period. The paint is so beautifully applied that it looks like it's about six inches deep.

The interior maintains a factory look with the addition of modern gauges in a traditional-looking instrument panel setting.

The unique Colorado Customs aluminum wheels fit well with the charisma of the 1931 Chrysler Imperial.

1934 PLYMOUTH RESTO-MOD

Keith Powers fell in love with this vintage Plymouth Resto-Mod when he first saw it three years ago. He liked it because it has a completely stock body, with the exception that the rear taillights are flared in.

It's also missing its bumpers, but that's a look that Keith likes. The turn signals are located low on the front side.

The power train has a modern flair with a 350 GM crate engine hooked to a modern Chevy automatic transmission. It came with that custom red shade. The 15-inch American Racing Wheels help fill the wheel wells.

Nestled in the small body-colored engine compartment is a 350 GM Crate Engine pumping out 300 horses. It makes this vintage Plymouth squat down and go!

Although missing the bumpers (a common practice), the remainder of this 1934 Plymouth Resto-Mod has its stock grille, lights and hood louvers.

The suspension system was totally upgraded with a Mustang II front end with coil-over shocks while there are late-model Posey leaf springs in the rear. The interior is impressive with custom tan-colored modern buckets, power windows and door locks and VDO black-faced gauges.

Builder and owner: Keith Powers

The interior has been given a nice custom touch with a tan decor and modern vinyl bucket seats, VDO black face gauges, a tilt wheel and custom steering wheel. The dash is done in body color.

1935 CHEVY COUPE RESTO-MOD

This classy little 70-plus-year-old Chevy coupe illustrates the best of "Resto-Modding" a vintage vehicle.

The power train possesses a modern General Motors 350 crate engine that can push this Bowtie coupe down the road in a hurry. The remainder of the power train isn't new, but the modern Turbo 400 tranny and newer Chevy rear end play beautifully together.

The suspension has been modernized with an independent front end. The front disc brakes provide excellent stopping power.

This 1935 Chevy Resto-Mod shows its stock body to great advantage. That's 1995 Caddy Metallic Red paint. The bumpers have been eliminated as is the case with many of these build-ups. There are three wooden strips on each of the running boards.

Power is greatly upgraded with the addition of this modern General Motors 350 crate engine that replaced the 305-cid V-8 that was in place when the purchase was made. It's nicely detailed in aluminum and chrome.

The interior has been modernized with VDO gauges, an IDIDIT steering column and Grant steering wheel, Vintage Air conditioning and the custom gray bucket seats.

The body is totally original but the bumpers have been eliminated front and rear. Those small red squares beneath the front fenders are actually the turn signals that this model certainly didn't have in its day.

Like any other Resto-Mod, the interior has been upgraded in an excellent manner with a number of aftermarket pieces.

This is an example of a relatively low-budget Resto machine, with owner Howard West indicating that it is probably in the low-$30,000 range.

Builder: Homebuilt by a previous owner
Owner: Howard West

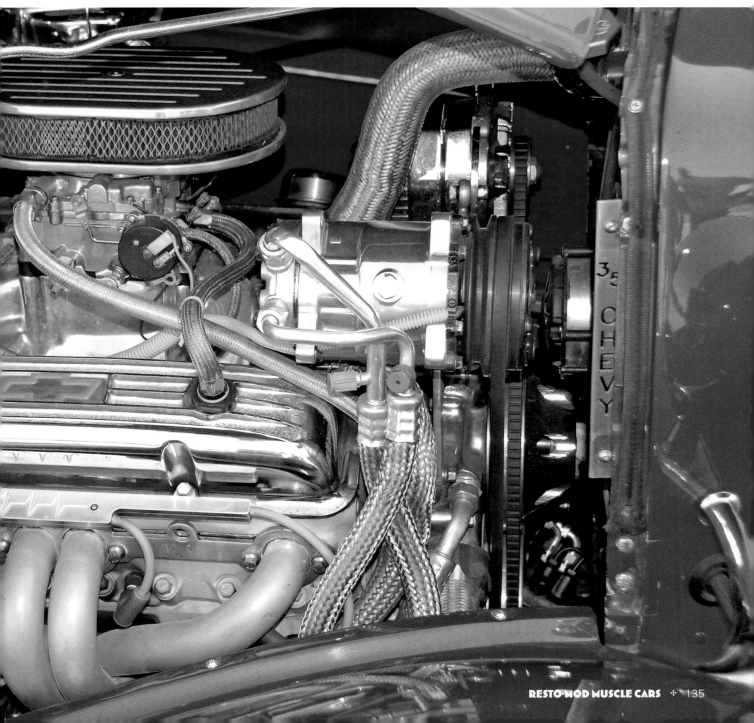

This red and dark purple 1937 Chevy Master Deluxe Resto-Mod is a low-budget effort with excellent results. It's set off with modern Eagle aluminum-spoked wheels.

1936 Chevy Master Deluxe

Owner Okey Smith explained that he had the car about four years before it was photographed. He explained the car was practically done when he got it, but he had added a number of modifications, did additional detailing and other items.

Smith said that it's a relatively low-budget effort with probably less than $30,000 involved. But it goes to show you don't need a six-figure investment to build a vehicle that's fun to display and drive.

The power train is newer by many decades with a 1980s 400-cid small block engine carrying an Edelbrock 450cfm four-barrel carb. It's nicely detailed in chrome and polished aluminum.

Other power train components include a 350 Turbo transmission with a shift kit and a modern rear end. It all drives 15-inch Eagle wheels. Driving is improved with the addition of a 1970 Nova front end with coil springs and disc brakes. The remainder of the underside is totally stock.

A gray and violet tweed covers just about everything inside including the dash. But what is also on that dash are modern VDO gauges, an Auto Meter Tach and a killer stereo system.

This Chevy is lots of Resto-Mod for reasonable dollars!

Builder: An unknown previous owner in collaboration with present owner Okey Smith

The engine is a 1980s Chevy 400 small block equipped with a B&M shift kit. There is a serious amount of chroming that has been done on the power plant.

The interior is covered in a gray and violet tweed material with 1997 Saturn bucket seats. The stock dash carries VDO gauges, a custom tilt wheel, and a Pyle Stereo.

The stock rear appearance is altered by deletion of the rear bumper, the chrome exhaust tips, the relocated modern slotted taillights and the brake light in the rear window.

1936 Ford Resto-Mod Coupe

Larry Kaminski sure has one tough-looking Resto-Mod creation with this all-steel 1936 Ford Coupe creation. Right off the bat, check out that glorious 1997 Nissan Beige paint scheme covering the totally stock body.

The only minor deviation was the builder moved the bumpers in closer to the body for a cleaner look. And those flashy 16- and 17-inch Billet Specialties wheels certainly aren't stock.

No vintage Flathead V-8 engine here— there's a modern 350-cid, 300-horse Chevy crate engine hooked to a Turbo 350 automatic tranny with a shift kit, a custom driveshaft and a 10-bolt Camaro rear end.

The suspension is modernized with a

The stock look is apparent from this three-quarter rear view. That gold-like appearance is actually a 1997 Nissan color, New Beige.

The builder of this 1936 Ford Resto-Mod is strictly a stock guy and explained that there had been absolutely no cutting of any kind on the body. It's carried by Billet Specialties wheels with 16-inch versions on the front and 17-inch rear wheels.

The custom interior features body color on the stock dash. A new gauge panel has been installed which contains modern white-face gauges.

straight, four-inch dropped front axle with Chassis Engineering shocks and leaf springs. Also, there are modern General Motors front disc brakes.

Nice touches abound in the upgraded interior with Eagle Premier power six-way bucket seats, a custom dash with modern gauges and a hidden custom stereo. The blue color scheme is continued in the trunk.

Owner: Larry Kaminski

The pedestals for the taillights have been shortened slightly and it also now carries a custom gas cap. Also, note the unusually shaped stock bumper which is identical to the front bumper.

1937 FORD RESTO-MOD SEDAN

This 1937 Ford sedan certainly sets the standard for the Resto-Modding of older models. The meticulous paint scheme gives it the look of a modified custom body, but that's not the case. That's pretty much the stock body!

Where most of the older-model Resto machines use modern, but not new, power plants, this seven-decade-old Ford has a new 350-cubic inch, 330-horsepower GM crate engine. It's hooked to a 350 Turbo automatic transmission and a modern nine-inch Ford rear end.

The classic design of this '37 Ford Sedan is greatly enhanced by the contrasting modern colors. With the exception of the shaved hood, the body is totally stock.

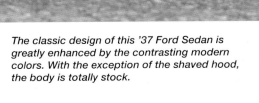

Modern power in the form of a 350/330 horse GM Crate engine makes for dependability and significant performance

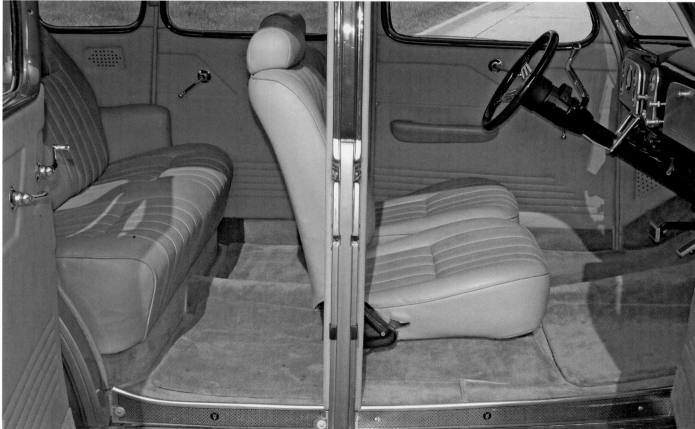

The stock rear hinging of the back door allows easy entrance and exit. The totally custom interior features modern seats, and pedals.

Suspension was also upgraded with a Heidts Suspension up front with aftermarket leaf springs and a beefy sway bar in the back end. It definitely drives like a dream.

It's perfection—what more can you say?

Owner: Jim Hasty

1940 Ford Deluxe Resto-Mod

Chuck Butts has proved that you can have a lot of fun with a quality Resto-Mod for only $20,000. Just check out this colorful (that's Bright Red and Peach) 1940 Ford Deluxe version.

He explained that it's all the original sheet metal and the interesting two-tone paint scheme really sets it off. Those are also the original bumpers and trim.

It's totally modern under the hood with a General Motors 350-cubic inch crate engine. The stock 300 horses are kicked up a little with an Edelbrock aluminum intake, a 600cfm carburetor and Hooker Headers.

The transmission is a modified 350 Turbo with a shift kit and a 10-bolt rear end. There's a 1970 Camaro front clip with coils, and the same donor vehicle providing the rear leaf springs.

The interior is nicely done with the stock dash painted in the red body color. The bucket seats came from a later-model Buick and there are modern VDO gauges. A 1979 Chevy provided the column and that same Buick donated its steering wheel.

Builder: A previous owner and current owner Chuck Butts

This 1940 Ford Deluxe Resto-Mod carries its classic stock body. Underneath, there is a 1970 Camaro front clip with coil springs up front and leaf springs in the rear.

The interesting color combination of red and peach sets this vintage resto version apart. Notice that all the chrome and handles have been retained.

Power comes from a GM 350-cid, 300-horsepower crate engine. It's a bright montage of chrome and polished aluminum that gets a ton of attention.

They certainly didn't have bucket seats in 1940—late-model Buick seats now fill that void. Also inside are black-faced VDO gauges, a Moon Tach and a late-model Buick steering wheel.

1940 Ford Convertible Resto-Mod

When John Whip purchased this 1940 Ford convertible a number of years ago, it was a rusty basket case with no floorboards. "A number of guys had tried to fix it up, but they ended up screwing it up," he recalled.

The owner worked long and hard to create the magnificent Resto-Mod you see here, an excellent combination of the new and the old. Some minor refinements on the body really accentuate its classic design.

Whip will admit that he reverted to a late model Chevy engine replacement for economy reasons, along with a 350 Turbo and a Ford Granada eight-inch rear end.

There is no front bumper to detract from its stock appearance, but he says that will be coming along later.

The owner admitted, "I didn't want to build a hot rod from the car that would have been cut and tubbed. I wanted something that looked stock and was something that I could drive reliably down the road."

Builder and owner: John Whip

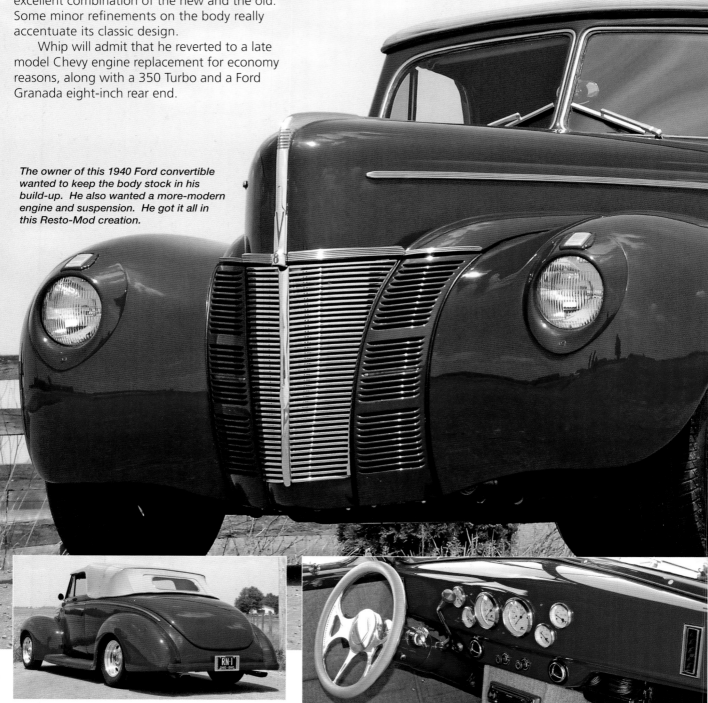

The owner of this 1940 Ford convertible wanted to keep the body stock in his build-up. He also wanted a more-modern engine and suspension. He got it all in this Resto-Mod creation.

The rear view shows the clean look of the body with its modern Corvette dark red enamel color. It's set off nicely with the 15-inch Centerline slotted wheels, about the largest that could be employed.

It's a thoroughly-modern interior done in tan tweed and body color, a '78 Chevy steering column, a custom steering wheel, billet handles, Dolphin white-face gauges and a hand-built console.

Amazingly, this beautiful 1941 Caddy Resto-Mod evolved from a rust bucket that was acquired in 1996.

1941 CADILLAC SERIES 62 CONVERTIBLE RESTO-MOD

This glorious 1941 Caddy, built to perfection by Gene Flaugher, brings the best of vintage and modern Cadillacs to the road.

Flaugher says he bought the car in 1996 and it was in terrible condition.

"About four inches of the bottom of the door had rusted away," he explained. He worked hard on the Cadillac for two years to bring it back to life.

The car runs with a 300-horsepower 1997 Cadillac 32-valve North Star 4.6-liter engine. It has been detailed to perfection giving it the appearance of a new engine. All the wires are hidden and an owner-fabricated upper engine shield was used.

It's hard to believe that beneath this modernistic owner-built engine housing is a 32-valve 1997 Caddy North Star 4.6-liter V-8. The remainder of the power train came from a 2000 Corvette.

A more-modern 350 Chevy small block provides about 300 horses to drive this classic Resto-Mod. It's detailed in chrome and body color.

The modern all-red leather interior is backed up with a Dakota Digital dash, a Lecarra steering wheel and a modern shifter.

The Laser Red paint scheme covers the almost-stock body. It's accented by the stainless steel running boards, the stainless steel horizontal trim stripes on each fender and the custom brake light between the trunk lid and the top boot.

The tranny is a modern Corvette 416D and the car also has a 'Vette rear end.

It took an ingenious cable system to make it all work. There are also 12-inch 'Vette disc brakes. The wheels are 17-inch six-spoke aluminum units. The Cadillac also has a modern front Corvette suspension under it.

The body is done in Laser Red with side body spears finished in stainless steel. The sheet-metal deviation is a third brake light from a Chevy Suburban. Owner and builder Flaugher fabricated a custom grille and added some running boards.

Then, there's that glorious interior done in a luxurious scarlet color. The custom dash carries Dakota Digital gauges and the Caddy is guided using a Lecarra steering wheel.

No doubt about it—this is an amazing machine to view!

Builder and owner: Gene Flaugher

Original touches like the chrome speed lines and hood ornament combined with modern paint and wheels make this one unique 1941 Cadillac convertible!

This rare 1948 De Soto Coupe has a grille that looks custom but is 60 years old. Be assured that owner Dave Rudy never had any intentions of changing the classic sheet metal. Its killer color is a 2002 GMC Envoy shade.

1948 DE SOTO RESTO-MOD

Owner Dave Rudy says his 1948 De Soto Resto-Mod is a real attention-getter wherever he shows it. It's a stunning combination of the old and new plus old school and high-tech. With the exception of a few refinements, the classic body is stock.

Then, there's that monster Viper engine under the hood. The remainder of the power train contains a six-speed Tremax unit and a 1978 Lincoln differential.

Power comes from the 21st century's Dodge Viper 460-cid V-8 hooked to straight-through exhaust pipes. And there is an aluminum intake manifold sitting atop this fuel-injected big-block powerhouse. It's detailed with chrome, polished aluminum and hidden wires.

The original interior has been retained with the addition of modern Dakota Digital gauges and touches like new floor pedals and other upgrades. The modern-style seats are covered in white lambskin.

The body remained very close to stock with minor changes including the shaved hood, the flip gas door and a three-inch drop in the rear—a height that can be adjusted. The large exhaust pipes can be seen emerging from underneath the rear bumper.

The car has modern four-wheel disc brakes. Much of that unique original dash has been retained, but digital gauges have been added.

"Showstopper" would be putting it mildly for this vintage De Soto Resto-Mod!

Builder and owner: Dave Rudy

The interior in this 1949 Mercury is highly customized with a white leather motif, a Smoothies steering wheel, Auto Meter white-face gauges and molded door panels.

Most of these models were chopped and channeled into low-slung hot rods. The owner of this 1949 Mercury was having none of that.

This '49 Mercury Resto-Mod has a near-stock external appearance with the exception of the vertical bar in the grille, the shaved hood and rear deck, deletion of the door handles and subtle light pinstriping. Also a new Mercury logo!

This monster 500-cid, 500-horsepower V-8 in this 1949 Mercury certainly doesn't look like the 1973 Caddy engine it is. The valve covers, intake manifold and air cleaner cover all carry an aluminum coating.

1949 AND 1950 MERCURY RESTO-MODS

Al Barry is into 1949 through 1951 Mercurys big time. But he's not into the expected chop-and-channel hot rod conversions.

That classic body stays intact with the Resto-Mod conversions he ac-complished. We're focusing on the two Mercurys he converted—a 1949 and a '50. Although they look considerably different, there are many similarities.

Both use 1973 Cadillac engines, Turbo 400 automatic transmissions, four-link Art Morrison frames, 12-inch Wilwood disc brakes, restored original gauges, Air Ride Technologies suspension systems and have other similar features.

The differences occur with body preparation, the '49 being nosed and decked with trim removed, while the '50 carries all the stock chrome. The engines are of different displacement, the 1949 carrying the 500-cid version while the 1950 has the 472-cid engine.

Two vintage Mercury Resto-Mods, so different and so much alike!

Owner: Al Barry

The 1973 Caddy engine in this '50 Mercury is more stock appearing than the 1949 version but it has been upgraded in performance with a Comp Cam and headers.

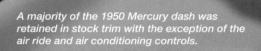

A majority of the 1950 Mercury dash was retained in stock trim with the exception of the air ride and air conditioning controls.

One year newer, this 1950 Mercury has a different look with the body chrome retained. With its low stance and wide white walls, this one definitely has a 1950s period look.

The stock flowing body lines and massive rear bumper and guard deserve to be retained, as the owner of this 1950 Mercury Resto-Mod did.

It was one of Ford's most popular models, and this 1950 Ford looks even better as a Resto-Mod. The color is very close to the original maroon shade. *Vanderhoof*

1950 FORD RESTO-MOD

One of Ford's popular postwar models was the 1950 Ford. It makes a nice Resto-Mod starting point, as this example reveals.

The power train, of course, is highly upgraded over the original with a modern 2003 small block that was pulled out of a vehicle that had been rolled over in a crash. Modern pieces are also in place with a 4R70W Ford automatic transmission and a Currie nine-inch 3.55 rear end.

The front suspension is a modern independent rack-and-pinion unit. The wheels are Coys 18 inchers on all four corners.

The interior is one of the highlights of the Resto with a Pro Woodgrain-detailed dash and modern digital gauges. P Jays did a magnificent job on the upholstery!

Builder: Just Dream'n
Owner: Dennis Vanderhoof

The engine in the 1950 Ford Resto-Mod is a modern one, a 2003 4.6-liter Mustang V-8. *Vanderhoof*

The rear of the Resto has been customized with the exhausts through cutouts on the lower part of the bumper. The trunk has been decked and those are custom taillights. *Vanderhoof*

The stock look is still in place but there is some wood-grain facing on part of it. There is a single digital dial and an aftermarket wheel wrap. The upholstery is leather. *Vanderhoof*

CHAPTER 9

MULTI-MODEL RESTO-MODS

The types of Resto-Mods covered by this chapter are a narrow niche in the hobby, but the vehicles that result are certainly interesting.

The construction techniques with these models actually combine the attributes of two or more models of different years to bring forth the best of both designs.

There are several ways of achieving this type of build-up that have been observed. First, there is the combining of sheet metal of different models and years to achieve an entirely different look.

Another technique that has been employed is to select a base model, completely remove the front and rear of the body and install the equivalent parts of a completely different model and model year.

Others have combined two models together for economic reasons. It might provide a different look, but the level of fabrication is also at a high level.

Maybe the most-unique 1950s Resto-Mod is this "789," a vehicle that incorporates parts of the 1957, 1958 and 1959 Chevys from front to rear. Its long, low streamlined look puts it in a sports-car category. n2a

789 CHEVY RESTO-MOD

So what in the heck do those three numbers mean in the name of this dramatic Resto-Mod? Well, that's easy. This n2a-built (for No Two Alike) machine is actually a combination of 1957, 1958 and 1959 Chevys. The amount of cutting, fitting and blending of vintage sheet metal boggles the mind!

The front, obviously comes from a 1957 Chevy while a 1958 is in the middle and those

familiar tail fins of the 1959 design are bringing up the rear. It all comes together in glorious fashion. Too bad Chevy didn't build such a design!

Everything about this machine is unique. It's like a fine piece of jewelry, possibly too fine to ever be driven. With this level of design and engineering, one can hardly wait to see what comes next from those innovative minds at n2a.

Builder: n2a Motors

The three years of design integrate beautifully along the sides of the "789" Resto-Mod.   n2a

The interior takes on a modern look with a Corvette interior. It also has a 200 mph speedometer.   n2a

It's definitely 1959 at the rear using that year's distinctive Chevy deck with the characteristic tear-drop taillights and those patented fins.   n2a

The more you look at this Resto-Mod, the more it keeps you guessing. It comes down to the fact that it's a combination of a 1949 Ford and a 1996 Thunderbird.

The 17-inch ASA five-spoke aluminum wheels support low-profile Kumho Ecsta tires.

1949 Ford/1996 T-Bird Resto-Mod

Owner Bill Ostermeyer says this unique restoration has been called a "1949 Thunderbird." And there is a lot of 1996 T-bird here that was the donor vehicle for this build-up. The front and rear of the T-bird was removed and replaced with 1949 Ford replica pieces. The result was that vintage look, but with the modern interior.

The 4.6-liter T-Bird engine is a far cry from the Flathead V-8 engine normally associated with the 1949 Ford. The minimal changes to the vintage Ford look are 1950 Ford back-up lights and a Ford Fusion brake light. The driving is aided with the T-Bird's automatic transmission, four-wheel disc brakes and Eibach coil-over shocks. You better believe that there are gawks by the ton, with that wondering look of "What the heck is it!"

Builder and owner: Bill Ostermeyer

The vintage lines of the '49 Ford are still in place here, but they have been enhanced with the custom taillights, higher rear stance and larger rear wheel cut-outs.

1956 FORD F-150 PICKUP RESTO-MOD

Looking at this outstanding 1956 Ford pickup Resto-Mod, there is no evidence about how it evolved. When you learn how it happened, you will be amazed.

Owner Tom Harber explained, "This Ford pickup body sits atop a 1989 Lincoln Mark IV chassis. Those two parts would seem to be incompatible, but after a huge amount of cutting and piecing, it was accomplished to perfection."

The builder of this very-cool Resto-Mod is unknown.

After the two were joined, the old F-150 immediately adopted all the advanced suspension, interior and power train of the luxury Lincoln. The owner explained that it feels just like he's driving that Mark IV. In effect, he is!

Even though the interior is pure Lincoln, the builder decided to carry some of the body color inside. He did it by coloring the door panels and dash in the exterior Salmon.

Builder: Unknown
Owner: Tom Harber

A monster Lincoln 460-cid power plant provides about 400 horsepower. Even in its stock trim, it still speaks of a lot of muscle.

The donor '89 Lincoln Mark IV provided the doors, seats and other items in the modern-appearing interior. The dash sports modern Dolphin black-face gauges.

Even though this 1956 Ford F-150 pickup has a modern paint scheme, it hasn't lost it's original look.   Wickett

1939 Graham/1997 Ford Crown Victoria/1997 Lincoln Mark VIII Resto-Mod

Even though this Resto-Mod can be identified as a 1939 Graham from the outside, there's certainly a lot more to it than that. There were parts from three different models that were blended together to get this amazing result.

The 1939 Graham body was slightly modified with stylish running boards. The chassis came from a 1997 Ford Crown Victoria. Finally, the interior, power train and roof came from a Lincoln Mark VIII. The level of complexity used to integrate these three different entities is mind-bending and was accomplished with a high level of perfection.

Builder: Ed Jamison
Owner: Tom Gerdes

The modern Town Car interior had to be reconfigured to fit. A custom console was added with the contained instrumentation aimed toward the driver. The Colorado Customs steering wheel design parrots the wheel design.

The width of the Graham was increased by three inches to accommodate the Crown Victoria frame. The all-steel body-color running boards were also added. The interesting position of the taillights is original.

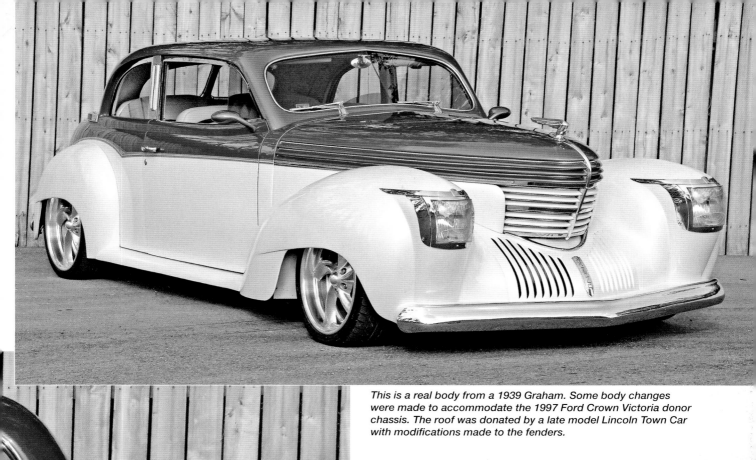

This is a real body from a 1939 Graham. Some body changes were made to accommodate the 1997 Ford Crown Victoria donor chassis. The roof was donated by a late model Lincoln Town Car with modifications made to the fenders.

The modern 32-valve Lincoln engine provides ample size to power this beauty. In order to fit in the engine compartment, it had to be set back eight inches.

CHAPTER 10
RESTO-MOD CONSTRUCTION

The building of Resto-Mods is just about as varied as the multitude of Resto-Mod styles that exist today. This chapter will examine the ever-growing industrial base that supports the hobby. It is impossible to fully identify all of them, but they are out there in force.

There are individuals building Resto-Mods in ever-increasing numbers. For the most part, they are lower-budget build-ups, but that doesn't mean that many of them aren't lacking in quality. Some of the homemade Resto-Mods highlighted in this book were constructed for $20,000 or less, and in some cases, much less.

Many of the Resto-Mod builders started out crafting street machines and hot rods before turning to these models of the 21st century. With the exception of the continuation car builders, covered in Chapter 3, a majority of the Resto-Mods are one-off machines.

A large percentage of the vehicles come as a result of a customer's request to make the conversion to his personal car. Some Resto-Mods see a minimal conversion, possibly leaving the interior untouched, others are built up to the hilt with the final tab possibly reaching into the six-figure category.

Other shops doing Resto-Mod fabrication might build them with the modifications being the choice they felt would attract prospective buyers. Some of these shops might concentrate on one car at a time, while others might have several build-up operations going on simultaneously. There is no template for Resto-Mod construction practices.

Just as different are the techniques used to reach the final product. The normal technique is to start with an existing car and completely modify it with the expected modern power train, suspension system and undercarriage along with an upgraded interior.

But in recent years, the Resto-Mods have continued to become wilder and wilder, and it follows that the construction is also more challenging. A new trend is actually the joining together of two different vehicles.

The body used is the selected look of the vehicle, usually a 1950s through 1970s model. And with the continuing production of Resto bodies, you no longer need to find a correct body for your Resto-Mod. These new bodies are exactly correct, and if you are interested in building a vintage Mustang or Camaro Resto, one of these might be a good choice. It is also almost a certainty that more of these body styles will continue to be produced.

Once the body is selected, a complete chassis from a completely different (and more modern) model is rolled beneath it. Then the fun begins with the tedious—and often difficult—process of making everything fit together. The difficulty is due to the number of decades in age separating the two models.

Some of the examples that have been noted with these build-ups are integrating a late model Viper with V-10 power beneath a 1960s Mopar body such as a Challenger or 'Cuda.

Another recent effort noted was joining a 1950 Chevy body and a much later IROC Camaro. Once completed, the Resto-Mod takes on a completely different aura with that modern interior and performance under the vintage hood.

Still another technique is to use a modern machine as the vehicle's base. The front and rear body panels are removed and replaced with vintage sheet metal. The resulting vehicle appearance is interesting, to say the least.

An example of that technique was integrating a 1990s-model Thunderbird and 1949 Ford pieces. Today, there is even a kit that enables such a Resto-Mod conversion.

A look at the businesses that construct Resto-Mods—check the appendix—provides an idea of the number of companies that exist. Those numbers continue to grow. An interesting observation about these firms is that many concentrate on just one of the Big-Three models.

Even though the level of construction for this type of vehicle is difficult, many still are completed in garages by single builders. Quite frankly, the Resto-Mod trend is growing and certainly has the potential to reach even greater heights.

With all the different philosophies in Resto-Mod construction, there seems to be one constant. It is that the vintage bodies used are maintained in close-to-stock trim. Sure, there will be considerable smoothing, but those familiar lines will still be in evidence. Some builders remove the door handles and trim, but that's about it.

The following is a discussion of many of the major parts and pieces that are finding their way into the building of today's Resto-Mods.

RESTO-MOD BODIES

Today, Resto-Mod creations are still using the original factory bodies, but the time will come in the near future that the junkyards have been totally cleaned out and the bodies from low-powered versions of the classics have been used. For example, six-cylinder versions of the 1967 and '69 Camaros would fall into that category.

If you are starting with an older car for your Resto-Mod creation, most shops will tell you to take the body down to bare metal, repairing the rust and dents before painting takes place.

The ultimate preparation, shown here with this body, is the blasting operation—done with sand, shells, beads, soda or other media. It removes all impurities that remain in crevices. It also removes all traces of rust.

The painting of a Resto-Mod is the same operation that is accomplished on the restoration of an original car. This particular paint operation shows the painting of the 1970 Buick GSX shown in Chapter 4.

It's not surprising to read in today's trader magazines that people are looking for vintage Camaros, Chevelles, Impalas and other classics "in any condition."

Did you ever wonder what they are planning on doing with them?

Several companies have provided the answer with complete and totally correct stock bodies for certain popular models. This could allow the Resto-Mod craze to last indefinitely.

Dynacorn Classic Bodies Inc., for example, is one of the leaders in this area with a 1969 Camaro coupe body that includes the trunk and both doors. In 2006, the company also introduced a 1967 Mustang fastback body—a very popular addition with Ford fans.

Dynacorn has also addressed the vintage truck fans with a 1947 through 1950 Chevy pickup cab replacement shell assembly that includes the doors. A Dynacorn official indicated that 15 years ago it wasn't possible to build these bodies because the technology wasn't available. Today, that's no longer the case.

The Retro Rides Company, in association with Goodmark Industries, is building 1967 Camaro bodies that will mate with late model Camaro floor pans, chassis and running gear. Those are the makings of a Resto-Mod!

Here is how it works. Retro Rides starts out with an original early Camaro body and replaces any worn panels using Goodmark sheet metal. The Camaro body retains its cowl and A-pillars, including its original VIN tag. For titling purposes, it's still a 1967 Camaro. If you decide to perform the Resto-Mod procedure on an early Camaro or Firebird, this is one approach that can be taken.

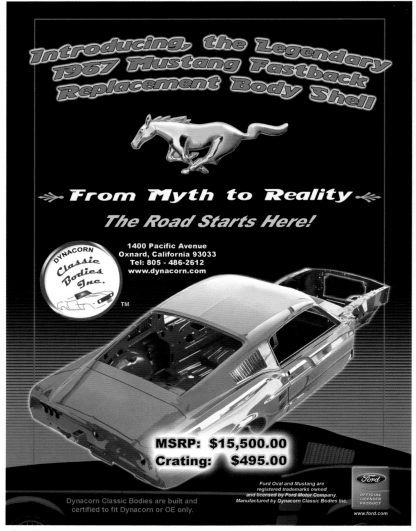

This Dynacorn advertisement shows the 1967 Fastback Mustang the company is offering. Dynacorn

This photo shows a number of the truck cab shells and 1969 Camaro bodies stored after production by Dyancorn. Dynacorn

The majority of the operations that produce Resto-Mods can make them to the requirements of the customer or build a version they think looks good and will sell. Shown here is an evolving 1955 Chevy Resto-Mod at Last Chance Garage and Body Shop near Dayton, Ohio.

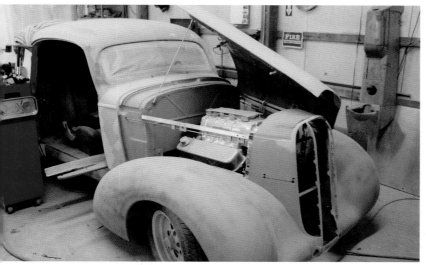

The popularity of older-model Resto-Mods is quite high. Here, a vintage sedan is under restoration and will eventually carry the expected upgraded power train, suspension and interior.

In this Resto-Mod build-up, the engine has been placed in position. Note the twin-turbo set-up of the power plant.

K.A.R. Auto Group Inc. has gotten into the classic-body business with a 1957 Chevy Bel Air convertible all-steel body, plus bodies placed on chassis.

The steel body-only option includes a heavy-gauge, spot-welded metal shell with fenders, quarters, braces, pans and the convertible-top bow assembly. The second option includes an Art Morrison Chassis—that is a Resto-Mod favorite—under the body, with or without suspension components.

YearOne is also a respected provider of classic sheet-metal parts and pieces.

RESTO-MOD ENGINES

The Resto-Mod power plants are about as diverse as the vehicles themselves. The accepted definition for a Resto-Mod engine is that they are "modern" and that has been interpreted in several ways.

First comes the use of an existing engine from a modern vehicle. That concept is fairly common. For example, many Resto-Mods use 1990s through 2000s Chevy LS-series engines from existing models.

The particular engine used in a Resto-Mod can evolve in several ways. You can start from scratch, as this aluminum block indicates, upgrade an existing engine or go with a modern crate engine. It's your choice. *Dynacorn*

In the Resto-Mod procedures done on older vehicles, the use of a new engine is rare. The usual technique involves the use of a "more modern" engine. In most cases, that means three-or-four decades newer.

With the top-line Resto-Mod conversions, the use of crate engines is an accepted procedure. Each of the Big-Three automakers has engines that are excellent choices for these applications.

For Ford, it's Ford Racing Performance Parts. General Motors fans can contact GM

This GM Performance crate engine chart shows the variety of engines that are available, from 454- to 572-cubic inches and from 425 to 720 horsepower. *GM*

Performance Parts. The Chrysler Corp. crowd can choose Mopar Performance Parts.

Many engine builders construct their own versions of crate engines that also are used in numerous Resto-Mod applications.

Other ways of achieving updated reliable performance takes place when an older engine is completely redone and built-up with modern parts.

When you are building a Resto-Mod, there is the possibility of installing a new crate or upgraded engine into a vintage machine. With the new crate engines, the builders thought about the Resto-Mod applications.

An example would be the installation of a new Mopar Performance crate engine in a vintage A-body version. You might think it would be a tough task, but the crates are designed for amazingly easy installation.

The engine arrives in complete condition including all the wiring and accessory drives. Also, the engine motor mounts are specifically engineered for this type of application. Another factor is the engines are also compatible with many vintage transmissions.

This nifty 5.0-liter Ford Cammer crate engine would be an addition to a Mustang Resto-Mod. Like many of the crate engines, this example is fuel injected. *Ford*

Still another engine family that has received attention in Ford Resto-Mod build-ups is the numerous modular engines. They started appearing in Ford production vehicles in the early 1990s. The most popular are the 4.6-liter, two-valve, single-overhead-valve versions.

Later versions of this engine type came in the mid-1990s with four-valve and three-valve dual overhead cam versions. They are popular choices for the Ford Resto-Mod enthusiasts.

Note that there are some clearance problems with the overhead cam versions when an installation is planned for a classic Ford. In that kind of undertaking, the problem occurs because of the high-mounted shock towers on those vehicles.

A characteristic of Resto-Mod engines is the elaborate serpentine belt system that hooks up all the pulleys with a single belt.

If a Ford crate engine is your bag, there are some nice choices available. For example, there are 300- and 400-horsepower versions of the 4.6-liter three-valve engine that is provided by Ford Racing.

As far as General Motors is concerned, there are two letters—LS—that define its recent engine program. It all started in the late 1990s when the LS1 5.7-liter version was introduced. Larger versions would follow reaching up to seven liters—with the Corvette LS7—and 505 horsepower.

Crate versions of the LS1, LS2 and LS7 engines also are available from GM Performance Parts. Another crate engine that will excite Resto-Mod builders is the L92 6.2-liter Escalade all-aluminum engine providing 403 horsepower.

This image shows the moly frame construction that offers rigidity as well as strength and flexibility to handle the engine's torque and the designated exhaust system's nooks and curves.

Some of the modern chassis for current high-end Resto-Mods incorporate square-tube chrome moly devices. The extra strength is needed to accommodate the high-power engines that are being used.

RESTO-MOD CHASSIS/SUSPENSION

If big money is being invested in one of these vehicles, it certainly doesn't make much sense to use the existing chassis.

Custom versions come into play, with a number of companies providing the complete system. Today, it's possible to purchase the complete front sub-frame that includes coil-over shocks, springs, disc brakes, control arms, sway bars and stabilizer bars. Also, a number of companies provide the complete rear four-link suspension systems.

Many of those four-link systems are direct bolt-in units with no cutting of the floor required. Some of the systems also allow tying the front and rear together with sub-frame connectors. That makes a single very strong frame system. And with some of the engines that are being used, that strength is needed to handle the big-time torque they possess.

Scott's Hotrods 'n Customs provides direct bolt-on sub-frames for first-generation Camaros and Firebirds and a partial clip for second generation F-Cars. The popular Resto-Mod LS engines bolt in with little trouble.

If you want to go whole hog, there are complete front and rear suspension packages available for certain models. Some of these systems have adjustments applicable to the building of Resto-Mods. Included are adjustable stances, both front and rear, and mounts for any engine or transmission.

For example, Art Morrison has a complete chassis that is a bolt-in replacement for the OEM 1955 through 1957 Chevy chassis with no welding required. The frame even includes bumper and body mounts and it can accommodate any automatic or manual transmission.

This advanced chassis incorporates square tubing, a modern sway bar, coil-over shocks and other innovations.

RESTO-MOD TRANSMISSIONS

The trend in Resto-Mod transmissions seems to be heading toward the modern and sophisticated five- and six-speed units.

By far, the Tremec versions are the most popular. If you are economically enabled, you might want to look at using a modern tranny that is built to handle the modern power plants.

It should be noted, though, that when a newer transmission is installed, there is the likelihood of clearance problems. There are times when some metal might need to be trimmed in a particular area. Other solutions have involved mounting the transmission further forward or rearward, or higher or lower. Those required moves, however, would also cause the engine position to be slightly altered.

RESTO-MOD APPEARANCE ASPECTS

One aspect that is extremely important to a modern Resto-Mod is that curbside appearance. Builders explain that the body finish is the big key. They advise owners to spend as much time as possible to get that ultimate finish.

It seems that the Tremec transmission is the standard for the Resto-Mods of the 21st Century. The Tremec is the brand of choice in a large number of examples in this book. Tremec

One characteristic that all Resto-Mods share is a set of large dramatic wheels. Here is just a sample of the types that are available.

With any sharp Resto-Mod, you just gotta have a sharp steering wheel. Grant manufactures some of the best, including the one shown here. Grant

Particular attention should be directed to areas of the body that may have been slightly altered, areas where the curve of a piece of sheet metal has been turned just a little more than the factory angle.

But with today's Resto-Mods, the underside needs to look just as good as the topside. You will see chrome and polished aluminum parts down there completely out of sight. That might be a little further than you want to go with your Resto, but it's becoming a definite part of the hobby.

Perhaps the most striking part of a modern Resto-Mod is when the hood is raised. With many RMs, when the sun hits that engine compartment, the reflection is blinding. Huge amounts of money are spent for chrome and polished aluminum to cover the engine. But again, if you can't afford that investment, many consider a stock engine that is detailed cleanly back to near-factory specs an impressive sight.

Professional Resto builders caution that the engine compartment needs to be painted before the engine is installed. Most Restos today have their engine compartment painted in body color, a popular technique that Chrysler used during the muscle years of the 1960s and 1970s.

The modern paints with their striking colors flow brightly on vintage sheet metal. But for some, they would just as soon repaint the body back to its original shade.

Inside, it's pretty much up to the builder about what is desired. Of course, almost every Resto-Mod sports different and newer seats, and a vast majority of the time the choice is bucket seats. Sure, it would be nice to have new buckets covered with leather. But you can go to a junk yard and get a nice set of 1980s or 1990s buckets, cover them with modern material and it will look super at a reasonable price.

Another noted trend that occurs with the dash refurbishment is to carry the body color to that surface. Modern gauges are a common touch, but many times they are installed in the stock dash and look really sharp. Otherwise, use your imagination!

The large, modern wheels are one expense that you are probably going to have to pay. But check in the trader magazines and see if you can find some used ones for sale. No need to pay full money for this item either.

CHAPTER 11
RESTO-MOD EXPOSURE

These Resto machines are appearing just about everywhere you look. The Resto-Mod look is getting to be big time and many will tell you that this could be the new muscle car of the 21st century. You can see the influence in a number of different venues.

This 1955 Chevrolet Bel Air two-door sedan is an example of the Resto-Mod touches including the combining of modern wheels and tires with the period body.

TOY CARS

One indicator of any new trend in the Resto-Mod area can be quickly noted in toy cars. And you better believe the Resto-Mod momentum is flat out! A look at the toy car shelves of many of the large retailers verifies that.

In fact, a recent look showed that a high percentage of the die-cast models were looking very much like the Resto-Mods. There are a number of companies devoted to that look completely.

One of the biggest companies is Jada Toys. It has several Resto-Mod-style series including Dub City Customs, Dub City Heat and Bigtime Muscle. The PRD Mark Company has a pair of Resto series with the Bad Ride and Blown sets. There are also a number of Chip Foose creations built under the Foose Design nametag, including a Full Throttle series.

The giant Mattel Toy Company is also looking toward the Restos with a number of models being produced from its Hot Wheels brand. In addition, there are RM models coming from Maisto (with its Pro Rodz series) along with larger Resto models from the Fairfield Mint.

The Resto-Mod characteristics are very detailed in many of the models with hoods that open, engine compartments painted in body color and upgraded modern engines.

Although Chip Foose is best known for his Resto-Mod cars, this model shows he obviously also has an interest in converting pick-up trucks.

This excellent 1/64th diecast '69 Chevelle Resto-Model is typical of the excellent models Jada releases.

This Foose Design diecast shows a Resto-Mod racecar version of a '70 Camaro.

This Maisto Mod Rodz set shows a pair of Resto-Mods on the box ('55 Chevy Wagon and '69 Camaro) and four different-colored 1/24th resto '70 Dodge Challengers for sale.

You could almost call the hand-built Ford GT a Resto-Mod as it was copied from the 1960s Ford GT40 racecar. It sure got a lot of exposure when it was initially on display in showrooms.

MAGAZINES

To date, there isn't a pure Resto-Mod magazine, but you have to wonder how long it will be before it happens. But be assured that there are many of the top automotive magazines that are carrying articles on them.

Just to mention a few, there are *Hot Rod, Super Chevy, Ford Builder, Mopar Muscle, Mopar Collectors Guide,* and numerous others.

CAR DEALERSHIPS

As mentioned in Chapter 2, a number of the modern production vehicles definitely have that popular Resto-Mod look. One of the models that really exemplified that look was the Ford GT—a close replica of the 1960s GT40 racer. Those cars certainly got a ton of exposure when the model was introduced by the Ford Motor Co. in 2005.

SEMA SHOW EXPOSURE

Every year, the giant SEMA show held in Las Vegas provides a look at everything high performance automotive.

The Resto-Mod technique also happens in the engine compartment where plenty of chrome is used with either period engines or modern crate versions.

The companies with the high-end exhibits battle each other for that vital exposure for their particular product. And would you believe (of course you would) that many of them have a bright and shiny Resto-Mod sitting right out there for all to see? No better place to get exposure in the national car magazines, newspapers and even books like this one!

In the 2007 SEMA Show, for example, some of the Restos that were out there showing their stuff included a 1966 Pontiac Le Mans convertible at the Original Parts Group booth.

When one of the super Motion cars shows its face, you know that it will generate huge interest.

The Mr. Norm Dodge Dart Resto-Mod drag car received huge exposure at the 2007 SEMA Show where it was displayed.

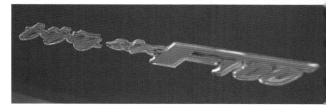

Often, a logo or chrome script is replaced with some type of custom paint treatment as this Resto-Mod logo reveals at close inspection.

Also, there was a Resto-Mod 1966 GTO at the Hot Wheels booth, and they were actually giving out a limited-edition model of the car that proved to be a very hot item.

At the Air Ride booth was a nifty 1962 Chevy "bubble-top" Resto, while OER had a silver and burgundy 1969 Camaro in Resto form. And there were many more.

Car Show Exposure

Go to any national or local car show these days and more times than not the featured cars could well be Resto-Mods. Just check out that gorgeous 1966 Chevelle that was a featured car in the 2005 Cavalcade of Customs show at Cincinnati. Also at the same 2007 show, a dramatic green 1969 Camaro Resto-Mod was in the spotlight and received huge attention from the crowd.

Auctions

Maybe the biggest exposure that the Resto-Mods get is on the national car auctions, a number of which get sweeping television coverage.

Some Resto-Mods have brought big numbers on the auction block. For example, a 1971 Hemi 'Cuda Resto-Mod brought about $80,000. A lot for sure, but just a small fraction of what the real item brought.

Also, at the Barrett-Jackson auction, a classy 1957 Chevy two-door with a 598-cid Chevy Merlin 1,000-horsepower mill with all the other expected ditties brought in a ground-pounding $176,000. Whether it was the exterior or the interior, it was all perfect.

The '50s Chevys have been hot items on the block. A 1955 Bel Air Resto with an LT1 'Vette engine brought a solid $104,500, while an LS7 505-horse 1957 Chevy Resto got huge money at $187,000.

Also at Barrett-Jackson, an interesting Resto version of a 1939 Lincoln Zephyr was a striking machine with a GM Vortec 5.3 liter, 275-horsepower fuel-injected engine paired with a GM 4l60E automatic transmission. Inside, there was a custom interior with leather seats, hand-fitted panels and air conditioning among the upgrades. It sold for $50,600!

Some of the most impressive muscle cars on the planet were the late-1960s and early-1970s 426 Hemi Challengers, 'Cudas and such. These machines are out of the ball park from a financial point of view. Many of them fall into the seven-figure category.

You can still get a Hemi machine, a Resto-Mod, for considerably less. For most, it's a viable alternative because there is still that vintage Mopar look. But the Hemi is a modern 5.7-liter version.

One of these Resto Mopar Hemis—a 1970 'Cuda to be exact—sold for $82,500 at Barrett-Jackson.

That's a lot, for sure, but compared to the price for the real thing, it's nothing!

At the Kruse International Auctions, there have been a number of Resto-Mods sold for big money. In its October 2006 event, a 1955 Chevy Resto-Mod brought an impressive $155,000.

It was an awesome machine with an injected Lingenfelter LS6 Chevy power plant hooked to a 4L60E transmission. The interior was a total custom creation. Boyd Coddington 17-inch wheels and modern Corvette disc brakes were just some of the impressive parts and pieces.

Another classy Kruse Resto offering was a 1956 Chevy with a modern Chevy LT1 engine, an electronic overdrive transmission and a new Curry Positraction rear end.

Other upgrades included power steering and brakes, billet pulleys and accessories, Billet Specialties aluminum wheels and Vintage Air climate control. Not as impressive as the previous 1955 Resto, this yellow-and-white stunner still brought $41,500.

Resto-Mods in National Advertisements

It just seems to be the trend in the first decade of the 21st century. Look at many national automotive advertisements and more likely than not, you will see a classy Resto-Mod machine staring back at you.

Just another bit of evidence of the popularity of the Resto-Mods. One can but wonder what's coming next!

This showpiece is a 1969 Boss 302 Mustang that has undergone the Resto-Mod treatment. Who knows what condition it was in before some talented people brought out its stunning beauty. *John Gunnell*

This 1971 Camaro Resto-Mod was recently seen on the block at the Russo and Steele Auction at Monterey, California. *Angelo Van Bogart*

RESTO-MOD SUPPORT

Builders/Designers

Aerocomp Performance
aerocompracing.com
407-330-7300

American Muscle Cars
americanmusclecars.com
909-381-7439

Autokraft
autokraft.org
715-874-5921

Baker's Vintage Automotive, Inc.
Bakersvintageauto@earthlink.net
937-209-4505

Baldwin-Motion
officialbaldwinmotion.com
941-957-0847

Blad Boys Muscle Cars
bladboysmuscle cars.com
937-429-4230

Blewetts Rod Shop
streetrodding.com
941-488-2377

Blue Moon Motorsports
bluemooncars.com
888-327-6747

BTO Cars
btocars.com
815-385-6286

Cars By Chris
kris@carsbykris.com
760-481-5542

Customs & Classic Restorations
chris@customsandclassics.com
801-288-1863

D&D Specialty Cars
customwebdesigns.biz
479-474-1114

Done Right Automotive Performance
donerightautomotive.com
715-693-5740

Fesler Productions
Feslerbuilt.com
602-953-8944

Foose Design
chipfoose.com

G-Force Design Concepts
gforcedesignconcepts.com
717-263-1994

Hot Rod Construction
hotrodconstruction.com
864-845-4545

Hills Automotive
hillsresto.com
740-944-2217

J2 Speed and Custom
j2speedandcustom.com
402-880-1402

K.A.R. Auto Group
karmustang.com
800-341-5949

Last Chance Garage and Body Shop
lcgarage.com
877-855-4992

Modern Muscle
modernmuscle.biz
276-666-1934

Mr. Norm's
Mrnorms.com
888-327-6747

Muscle Car Restorations
musclecarrestorations.com
715-834-2223

Performance West Group
performancewestgroup.com
760-630-0547

PFC Enterprises LLC
plumfloored@yahoo.com
816-739-0928

Prodigy Customs
prodigycustoms.com
407-832-1752

POR-15 Classic Restorations
porlscr.com
800-225-7422

Redline Autosports
jefferson@bryantmedia.us
405-880-5343

Reenmachine
reenmachine.com
805-648-7336

Ring Brothers Performance
ringbrothers.com
608-588-7399

Rod Rids by Troy
Rodrides.com
815-468-2590

RS Performance Concepts
roadstershop.com
847-742-1932

Schwartz Extreme Performance
schwartzperformance.com
815-455-2230 • 815-455-2233

Sean Hyland Motorsport
seanhylandmotorsport.com
519-421-2291

Superformance
superformance.com
800-297-6253

Ultimate Customs
Ultimateva.com
703-435-5000

Unique Performance
uniqueperformance.com
800-418-4543

YearOne
Yearone.com
770-493-6568

Yenko-Wildfire Garage
yenko-wildfire.com
814-227-2427

Bodies/Sheet Metal Pieces

The Paddock
paddockparts.com
800-428-4319

YearOne, Inc.
yearone.com
800-YEAR-ONE

Chassis

Art Morrison Ent., Inc.
artmorrison.com
866-558-1693

Crate Engines

Baldwin-Motion
originalbaldwinmotion.com

Bill Mitchell Hardcore Racing Products
theengineshop.com
631-737-0467

Blueprint Engines
blueprintengines.com
800-483-4263

Carolina Machine Engines
cmengines.com
800-903-6446

Dynacorn International, Inc.
dynacorn.com
805-486-2612

Edelbrock
edelbrock.com
800-416-8628

Ford Racing Performance Parts
fordracingparts.com
800-FOR-D788

GM Performance Parts
gmperformanceparts.com
810-606-2316

Golen Engine Service
golenengineservice.com
603-886-3800

HYE Tech Performance
chevyhiperformance.com
626-855-1154

Indy Cylinder Head Engines
indyheads.com
317-862-6300

Jon Barrett Hot Rod Engines
jonbarrett.com
800-342-6015

Katech Engines
katechengines.com
586-791-4120

Kenne Bell Engines
kennebell.net
909-941-6646

Keith Craft Racing Engines
keithcraft.com
870-246-7460

Machine Tech Racing Engines
machinetechracing.com
760-434-4935

Magnuson Products
magnusonproducts.com
805-642-8833

Mopar Performance Parts
mopar.com
588-755-9491

Pace Performance
paceperformance.com
330-652-5855

Potter Automotive
cadillacperformanceparts.com
423-332-7636

Ray Barton Racing Engines
raybarton.com
610-693-5700

Roush Performance
roushparts.com
800-59-Roush

Scoggin-Dickey Performance Parts
sdpc2000.com
800-456-0211

Sean Hyland Motorsport
seanhylandmotorsport.com
519-421-2291

Shafiroff Race Engines and Components
shafiroff.com
800-295-7142

Carroll Shelby Enterprises
carrollshelbyent.com
310-538-2914

Smeding Performance
smedingperformance.com
916-638-0899

Speed-O-Motive Inc.
speedomotive.com
626-869-0270

Street & Performance
hotrodlane.cc
479-394-5711

Turnkey Engine Supply
turnkeyengine.com
760-941-2741

World Products
worldcastings.com
631-981-1918

YearOne
yearone.com
770-493-6568

Dash Boards

Wabbits Dashes & Accessories
wabbitsww@aol.com
281-592-1211

Rocky Mountain Dashes
rockymountaindashes.com
719-302-0678

Exhaust Systems

Borla Performance Ind.
borla.com
877-462-6752

SLP Performance Parts
slponline.com
732-349-2109

Corsa Performance
corsaperf.com
800-486-0999

Billy Boat Performance Exhaust
bbexhaust.com
888-228-7435

Bassani Xhaust
bassani.com
866-782-3283

Gauges

Auto Meter Products, Inc.
autometer.com
815-895-8141

Headers

JBA Performance Exhaust Co.
jbaheaders.com
800-830-3377

Interiors

Classic Automotive Interiors
classicautomotiveinteriors.com
800-624-7460

Ignition Systems

MSD Ignition
msdignition
915-857-5200

Radiators

Griffin Thermal Products
griffinrad.com
800-722-3723

Be Cool Radiators
becool.com
888-243-2999

Rear Ends

Currie Enterprises
currieenterprises.com
714-528-6917

Dana Corporation
engineparts.com
800-338-8786

Moser Engineering, Inc.
moserengineering.com
269-726-4159

Strange Engineering
strangeengineering.net
847-663-1701

Serpentine Systems
Billet Specialties
billetspecialties.com
866-317-5937

Conceptone
conceptpulleys.com
877-889-0881

March Performance Pulleys and Brakes
marchperf.com
888-729-9010

Shocks

QA1 Precision PRoducts, Inc.
qa1.net
800-721-7761

Steering Wheels

Lecarra
wheeljungle.com

Stopping

Baer Incorporated
brakes@baer.com
602-233-1411

Master Power Brakes
mpbrakes.com
888-351-8785

SSBC
info@ssbrakes.com
800-448-7722

Wilwood Engineering
wilwood.com
805-388-1188

Suspension Systems

Air Ride Technologies
ridetech.com
812-481-4772

Eibach Springs
eibach.com
800-507-2338

Fat Man Fabrications
fatmanfab.com
704-545-0369

Just Suspension
justsuspension.com
800-872-1548

Jim Meyer Racing
jimmymeyerracing.com
800-824-1752

Ron Morris Performance
ronmorrisperformance.com
209-605-1590

Total Control Products
totalcontrolproducts.com
800-722-2269

Tires

Diamond Back Classic Radials
dbtires.com
888-922-1642

Dunlop Tires
dunloptires.com

Kumho Tires
kumhousa.com
1-800-HI KUMHO

Michelin Tires
michelin.com

Toyo Tires
toyo.com
888-541-1777

Transmissions

Muncie
muncie5speeds.com
561-743-4600

Phoenix Transmission Products
phoenixtrans.com
866-shiftup

TCI-Torque Converters
tciauto.com
800-PRO-XTCI

Tremec Transmissions
tremec.com
800-401-9866

Wheels

American Racing Wheels
Americanracing.com

Billet Specialties
billetspecialties.com
866-317-5937

Boyd Coddington
boydcoddington.com
888-254-3400

Bonspeed Forged Wheels
uswheel.com

Budnik Wheels
budnik.com
714-892-1932

Champion Motorsport
championmotorsport.com
800-775-2456

Colorado Custom
coloradocustom.com
562-602-0080

Crager Wheels
wheelcars.com

Fesler Designs
feslerdesigns.com
602-953-8944

Flaming River
flamingriver.com
866-822-1627

Halibrand Wheels
halibrand.com
760-598-1960

HRE Wheels
hrewheels.com

Intro Custom Wheels
introwheels.com
800-45-INTRO

NAD Wheels
nadwheels.com
714-282-0088

Specialty Wheels, LTD
specialtywheelsltd.com
503-491-8848TD

Stockton Wheel
stocktonwheel.com
800-395-9433

Performance Wheels
tdperf.com
513-671-4100

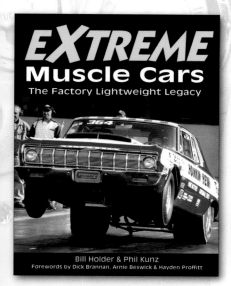
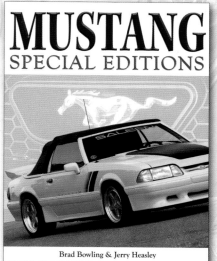
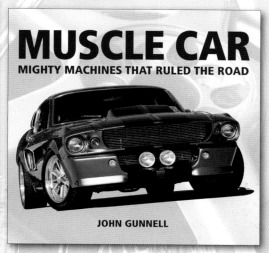
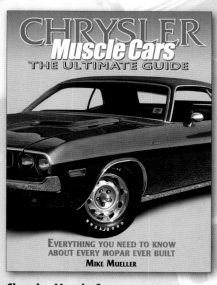
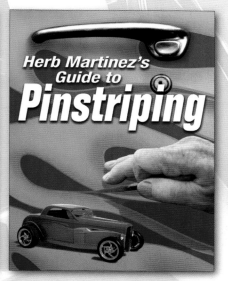